WeightWatchers®
in 20 minutes
250 Fresh, Fast Recipes

WILEY

John Wiley & Sons, Inc.

For general information on our other products and services or to obtain technical support please contact our Customer Care Department within the U.S. at 877-762-2974, outside the U.S. at 317-572-3993 or fax 317-572-4002.

Wiley also publishes its books in a variety of electronic formats. Some content that appears in print may not be available in electronic books. For more information about Wiley products, visit our web site at www.wiley.com.

ISBN 978-1-118-55277-3 (paper)

Weight Watchers Publishing Group

VP, Editorial Director: Nancy Gagliardi

Creative Director: Ed Melnitsky

Food Editor: Eileen Runyan

Editor: Deborah Mintcheff

Photo Director: Deborah Hardt

Managing Editor: Diane Pavia

Photography: Dasha Wright

Food Styling: Michael Pederson

Prop Styling: Karen Quatsoe

Assistant Editor: Katerina Gkionis

John Wiley & Sons, Inc.

Publisher: Natalie Chapman

Executive Editor: Anne Ficklen

Senior Editorial Assistant: Heather Dabah

Senior Production Editor: Amy Zarkos

Art Director: Tai Blanche

Cover Design: Suzanne Sunwoo

Interior Design and Layout: Joel Avirom and Jason Snyder

Manufacturing Manager: Kevin Watt

Printed in the United States of America

10 9 8 7 6 5 4 3 2 1

Cover photo: Chicken with Cremini Mushroom–Port Sauce (page 130)

About Weight Watchers

Weight Watchers International, Inc. is the world's leading provider of weight-management services, operating globally through a network of company-owned and franchise operations. Weight Watchers holds nearly 45,000 meetings each week worldwide, at which members receive group support and education about healthful eating patterns, behavior modification, and physical activity. Weight-loss and weight-management results vary by individual. We recommend that you attend Weight Watchers meetings to benefit from the supportive environment and follow the comprehensive Weight Watchers program, which includes a food plan, an activity plan, and a behavioral component. **WeightWatchers.com** provides subscription weight-management products, such as eTools and Weight Watchers Mobile, and is the leading internet-based weight-management provider in the world. In addition, Weight Watchers offers a wide range of products, publications (including **Weight Watchers Magazine** which is available on newsstands and in Weight Watchers meeting rooms), and programs for people interested in weight loss and control. For the Weight Watchers meeting nearest you, call **1-800-651-6000.** For information about bringing Weight Watchers to your workplace, call **1-800-8AT-WORK.**

Contents

Introduction

*W*eight Watchers is not about dieting—it's about living. And we at Weight Watchers are constantly striving to come up with new ways to help you maintain healthy eating habits that you will be eager to embrace every day.

In *Weight Watchers in 20 Minutes,* you will find 250 delicious dishes that will keep you on plan while keeping you in the kitchen for no more than 20 minutes. Alongside many of the recipes, you will find tips: the Time-Saver is all about smart, savvy ways of cutting down on your kitchen time without sacrificing flavor or quality, while Filling Extra suggests delicious healthy ways for you to make your meal more filling while staying on track to meet your goals.

The basis of our extraordinarily successful program remains the same: eating lean meats, poultry, and fish and plenty of fresh fruits and vegetables, while keeping fat and sugar to a minimum. Including whole grains, such as brown rice, bulgur, oatmeal, and whole-grain breads, pastas, and tortillas, as well as legumes, such as canned or dried beans and lentils, in your daily menu will help you stay satisfied longer. You'll find that you're eating food that tastes great and fills you up for fewer ***PointsPlus***® values than other foods.

So thumb through this beautiful volume of Weight Watchers recipes right away and get cooking—the rewards are many.

About Our Recipes

We make every effort to ensure that you will have success with our recipes. For best results and for nutritional accuracy, please keep these guidelines in mind:

- Recipes in this book have been developed for Weight Watchers members who are following Weight Watchers 360°. *PointsPlus* values are given for each recipe. They're assigned based on the amount of protein (grams), carbohydrates (grams), fat (grams), and fiber (grams) contained in a single serving of a recipe.

- Recipes include approximate nutritional information; they are analyzed for Calories (Cal), Total Fat, Saturated Fat (Sat Fat), Trans Fat, Cholesterol (Chol), Sodium (Sod), Carbohydrates (Carb), Sugar, Dietary Fiber (Fib), Protein (Prot), and Calcium (Calc).

- Nutritional information for recipes that include meat, poultry, and fish are based on cooked skinless, boneless portions (unless otherwise stated), with the fat trimmed.

- We recommend that you buy lean meat and poultry, and then trim it of all visible fat before cooking. When poultry is cooked with the skin on, we suggest removing the skin before eating.

- Before serving, divide foods—including any vegetables, sauce, or accompaniments—into portions of equal size according to the designated number of servings per recipe.

- Any substitutions made to the ingredients will alter the "Per serving" nutritional information and may affect the *PointsPlus* value.

- All fresh fruits, vegetables, and greens in recipes should be rinsed before using.

- All ◆Filling Extra suggestions have a *PointsPlus* value of *0* unless otherwise stated.

Rich and Creamy Oatmeal
with Blueberries and Walnuts

1

Welcome the Morning

Fruit and Cheese—Stuffed
French Toast

Mixed Berry French Toast

Raspberry-Cornmeal Pancakes

Brown Sugar—Banana Waffles

Lemon Pancakes with
Fresh Raspberry Sauce

Buckwheat-Applesauce
Griddle Cakes

Berry-Stuffed Cinnamon Crêpes

Strawberry and Sour Cream Blintzes

Pressure-Cooked Honey
and Spice Porridge

Oatmeal with Dried Fruit
and Brown Sugar

Spiced Oatmeal Brûlée

Rich and Creamy Oatmeal
with Blueberries and Walnuts

Fresh Fruit with Orange-
Scented Ricotta

Mango-Honey Breakfast Cooler

Mango-Peach Smoothie

Banana-Peach Protein Smoothie

Tropical Sorbet Smoothie

Denver Omelette

Provençal Vegetable Omelette

Potato and Green Pepper Frittata

Crab and Chive Frittata

Southwestern-Style Scrambled Eggs

Scrambled Eggs with
Smoked Salmon and Onion

Poached Eggs with Salsa
and Cheese

Mixed Vegetable Egg Foo Yong

Apple-Raisin Matzo Brei

Smoked Salmon, Dill,
and Red Onion Pizzas

Italian Salad Pizza

Microwave Sausage
and Chile Corn Bread

Turkey, Potato, and Sage Patties

Pinto Bean and Pepper Jack Burritos

Fruit and Cheese—Stuffed French Toast

SERVES 2

2 tablespoons light cream
  cheese (Neufchâtel), softened

4 slices whole-wheat bread

2 tablespoons strawberry or
  raspberry all-fruit spread

1 large egg

2 egg whites

3 tablespoons fat-free milk

1 teaspoon vanilla extract

½ teaspoon cinnamon

Pinch nutmeg

1 cup hulled and sliced
  strawberries

1 Spread the cream cheese evenly on 2 slices of the bread, leaving a ⅛-inch border. Spread the strawberry spread on the remaining slices of bread, leaving a ⅛-inch border. Put the slices of bread together to make 2 cream cheese–fruit sandwiches. Cut each sandwich in half on the diagonal; set aside.

2 Beat the egg and egg whites in a large shallow bowl or pie plate; whisk in the milk, vanilla, cinnamon, and nutmeg. Add 2 sandwich halves to the egg mixture; let stand until evenly soaked, about 20 seconds on each side. Repeat with the remaining 2 sandwich halves.

3 Spray a large nonstick skillet with nonstick spray and set over medium-high heat. Add the sandwiches to the skillet and cook until browned, 2–3 minutes on each side. Serve with the berries.

Per serving (2 sandwich halves and ½ cup strawberries): 321 Cal, 9 g Fat, 4 g Sat Fat, 0 g Trans Fat, 118 mg Chol, 427 mg Sod, 44 g Carb, 7 g Fib, 17 g Prot, 141 mg Calc. **PointsPlus** value: **8.**

Time-Saver

To soften the cream cheese in a flash, put it in a microwavable cup and microwave on High about 15 seconds.

Mixed Berry French Toast

SERVES 2

2 cups mixed berries, such as raspberries, blueberries, and small strawberries, hulled

1½ tablespoons sugar

1 teaspoon grated orange zest

2 large eggs

1 egg white

¼ cup fat-free milk

2 tablespoons orange juice

4 slices whole-wheat bread

1 Combine the berries, sugar, and orange zest in a serving bowl.

2 Beat the eggs, egg white, milk, and orange juice in a shallow bowl or pie plate. Add 1 slice of the bread to the egg mixture; let stand until the bread is evenly soaked, about 30 seconds on each side. Transfer to a plate. Repeat with the remaining 3 slices of bread.

3 Spray a large nonstick skillet with nonstick spray and set over medium-high heat. Add the soaked bread to the skillet, in batches if necessary, and cook until browned, 2–3 minutes on each side. Put 2 slices of French toast on each of 2 plates and top with some of the berry mixture. Serve the remaining berry mixture alongside.

Per serving (2 slices French toast and 1 cup berry mixture): 328 Cal, 9 g Fat, 2 g Sat Fat, 0 g Trans Fat, 213 mg Chol, 407 mg Sod, 50 g Carb, 7 g Fib, 16 g Prot, 128 mg Calc. *PointsPlus* value: **8.**

Raspberry-Cornmeal Pancakes

SERVES 4

1 cup reduced-fat baking mix

1 cup yellow cornmeal

1¼ cups low-fat (1%) milk

1 large egg, lightly beaten

3 tablespoons pure maple syrup

1 cup fresh or frozen raspberries

1 Combine all the ingredients except the raspberries in a medium bowl. Gently stir in the raspberries.

2 Spray a nonstick griddle or large nonstick skillet with nonstick spray and set over medium heat. Pour heaping ¼ cupfuls of the batter onto the griddle. Cook until bubbles appear and the edges of the pancakes look dry, 2–3 minutes. Turn and cook until golden brown, about 2 minutes longer. Transfer the pancakes to a plate and keep warm. Repeat with the remaining batter to make a total of 12 pancakes.

Per serving (3 pancakes): 341 Cal, 5 g Fat, 2 g Sat Fat, 0 Trans Fat, 56 mg Chol, 388 mg Sod, 64 g Carb, 4 g Fib, 10 g Prot, 136 mg Calc. **PointsPlus** value: **9.**

◆ *Filling Extra*

Sprinkle ½ cup fresh or thawed frozen raspberries over each serving of pancakes.

Brown Sugar—Banana Waffles

SERVES 4

⅔ cup whole-wheat flour

⅓ cup all-purpose flour

1½ teaspoons baking powder

½ teaspoon cinnamon

½ teaspoon salt

⅛ teaspoon nutmeg

1 ripe banana, cut into chunks

½ cup fat-free milk

1 tablespoon packed brown
    sugar

1 tablespoon canola oil

1 large egg

Honey or pure maple syrup
    (optional)

1 Preheat a waffle baker according to the manufacturer's directions.

2 Meanwhile, combine the whole-wheat flour, all-purpose flour, baking powder, cinnamon, salt, and nutmeg in a food processor; pulse to combine, about 3 seconds. Add the banana, milk, brown sugar, oil, and egg; pulse 3 times. Scrape down the sides of the bowl, then process until smooth, about 30 seconds longer.

3 When the waffle baker is ready, ladle in ½ cup of the batter. Close the lid and bake until the waffle is golden brown, about 2 minutes. Transfer the waffle to a plate and keep warm. Repeat with the remaining batter to make a total of 4 waffles. Serve with honey or maple syrup, if using.

Per serving (1 waffle without honey or maple syrup): 207 Cal, 5 g Fat, 1 g Sat Fat, 0 g Trans Fat, 54 mg Chol, 509 mg Sod, 35 g Carb, 4 g Fib, 7 g Prot, 162 mg Calc. **PointsPlus** value: **6.**

◆ Filling Extra

Top each waffle with ½ sliced small banana.

*Mango-Honey
Breakfast Cooler
(page 25);
Brown Sugar–
Banana Waffles*

Lemon Pancakes with Fresh Raspberry Sauce

SERVES 4

1 cup raspberries

¼ cup sugar + 2 tablespoons sugar

1 tablespoon lemon juice

1⅓ cups all-purpose flour

1 teaspoon baking powder

¼ teaspoon baking soda

¼ teaspoon salt

1 (8-ounce) container plain fat-free yogurt

½ cup fat-free milk

1 large egg

1 tablespoon canola oil

1 To make the raspberry sauce, combine the raspberries, ¼ cup sugar, and the lemon juice in a small saucepan and set over medium heat. Cook, stirring occasionally, until a chunky sauce forms, about 6 minutes. Transfer to a serving bowl; set aside.

2 To make the pancakes, combine the flour, 2 tablespoons sugar, baking powder, baking soda, and salt in a large bowl. Whisk together the yogurt, milk, egg, and oil in a small bowl. Add the yogurt mixture to the flour mixture, stirring just until combined.

3 Spray a nonstick griddle or large nonstick skillet with nonstick spray and set over medium heat. Pour scant ¼ cupfuls of the batter onto the griddle. Cook until bubbles appear and the edges of the pancakes look dry, 2–3 minutes. Turn and cook until golden brown, about 2 minutes longer. Transfer the pancakes to a plate and keep warm. Repeat with the remaining batter to make a total of 12 pancakes. Serve with the sauce.

Per serving (3 pancakes and about 3 tablespoons sauce): 334 Cal, 5 g Fat, 1 g Sat Fat, 0 g Trans Fat, 55 mg Chol, 423 mg Sod, 61 g Carb, 3 g Fib, 11 g Prot, 240 mg Calc. **PointsPlus** value: **8.**

Lemon Pancakes with
Fresh Raspberry Sauce

Buckwheat-Applesauce Griddle Cakes

SERVES 6

1 large egg

1 egg white

1 cup plain low-fat yogurt

½ cup unsweetened applesauce

1½ tablespoons canola oil

1 tablespoon pure maple syrup

¾ cup all-purpose flour

½ cup buckwheat flour

2 teaspoons baking powder

½ teaspoon salt

1 Beat the egg, egg white, yogurt, applesauce, oil, and maple syrup in a small bowl. Whisk together the all-purpose flour, buckwheat flour, baking powder, and salt in a large bowl. Add the yogurt mixture to the flour mixture, stirring just until combined.

2 Spray a large nonstick griddle or skillet with nonstick spray and set over medium heat. Pour ¼ cupfuls of the batter onto the griddle. Cook until bubbles appear and the edges of the griddle cakes look dry, about 2 minutes. Turn and cook until browned, 2–3 minutes longer. Repeat with the remaining batter to make a total of 12 griddle cakes.

Per serving (3 griddle cakes): 260 Cal, 8 g Fat, 2 g Sat Fat, 0 g Trans Fat, 56 mg Chol, 635 mg Sod, 41 g Carb, 3 g Fib, 9 g Prot, 224 mg Calc. **PointsPlus** value: **5.**

Time-Saver

The night before you plan to serve the griddle cakes, prepare the egg mixture and the flour mixture in separate bowls and cover. Refrigerate the egg mixture and leave the flour mixture on the counter.

Berry-Stuffed Cinnamon Crêpes

SERVES 4

1 cup mixed berries, such as raspberries, blueberries, and blackberries

2 teaspoons packed brown sugar

1 teaspoon lemon juice

1 large egg

⅔ cup fat-free evaporated milk

2 teaspoons granulated sugar

1 teaspoon unsalted butter, melted

¼ teaspoon salt

½ cup all-purpose flour

½ cup whole-wheat flour

½ teaspoon cinnamon

⅓ cup reduced-fat ricotta cheese

1 Gently toss together the berries, brown sugar, and lemon juice in a medium bowl; set aside.

2 To make the crêpes, beat the egg, evaporated milk, granulated sugar, butter, and salt in a large bowl. Whisk in the all-purpose flour, whole-wheat flour, and cinnamon until smooth.

3 Spray an 8-inch nonstick skillet with nonstick spray and set over medium heat. When a drop of water sizzles in it, pour in a heaping 2 tablespoons of batter, tilting the skillet to coat the bottom evenly with the batter. Cook until set on the bottom, about 30 seconds. Turn and cook until lightly browned, about 10 seconds longer. Slide the crêpe onto a sheet of wax paper. Repeat with the remaining batter to make a total of 8 crêpes, stacking them between sheets of wax paper.

4 Spread about 2 teaspoons of the ricotta in the middle of each crêpe and top with 2 tablespoons of the berry mixture; roll up each crêpe. Place 2 crêpes on each of 4 plates.

Per serving (2 filled crêpes): 238 Cal, 4 g Fat, 2 g Sat Fat, 0 g Trans Fat, 64 mg Chol, 240 mg Sod, 39 g Carb, 4 g Fib, 11 g Prot, 199 mg Calc. **PointsPlus** value: **6.**

◈ Filling Extra

Add an extra cup of berries to the berry filling. Save half of the filling for spooning over the crêpes.

Strawberry and Sour Cream Blintzes

SERVES 4

¼ cup orange juice

2 teaspoons lemon juice

2 tablespoons + 2 teaspoons sugar

1 pint strawberries, hulled and thickly sliced

½ cup reduced-fat sour cream

¼ teaspoon vanilla extract

4 (9-inch) ready-to-use crêpes

¼ teaspoon cinnamon

1 Combine the orange juice, lemon juice, and 1 tablespoon of the sugar in a medium saucepan and bring to a boil over medium heat. Cook until syrupy, 3–5 minutes. Remove the saucepan from the heat and stir in the strawberries. Set aside.

2 Combine the sour cream, vanilla, and 1 tablespoon of the sugar in a small bowl. Spoon 2 tablespoons of the sour cream mixture in the center of each blintze and fold in quarters. Combine the remaining 2 teaspoons sugar and the cinnamon in a cup. Sprinkle evenly over the blintzes and top evenly with the strawberry mixture.

Per serving (1 filled blintze and about ⅓ cup sauce): 204 Cal, 8 g Fat, 4 g Sat Fat, 0 Trans Fat, 55 mg Chol, 174 mg Sod, 29 g Carb, 2 g Fib, 6 g Prot, 112 mg Calc. **PointsPlus** value: **4.**

Time-Saver

Save time and use 2 (6-ounce) containers of blueberries or raspberries or 1 container of each, instead of hulling and slicing the strawberries.

Pressure-Cooked Honey and Spice Porridge

SERVES 8

4 cups fat-free milk

1½ cups Arborio rice

1 cup dark raisins

2 tablespoons honey

½ teaspoon cinnamon

¼ teaspoon nutmeg

¼ teaspoon salt

1 Combine all the ingredients in a pressure cooker and set over medium-high heat. Bring to a simmer, stirring constantly so the rice doesn't stick. Lock the lid in place and reduce the heat to medium. Bring the cooker to high pressure, following the manufacturer's directions. Cook for 6 minutes, adjusting the heat to maintain high pressure.

2 Use the quick-release method for releasing the pressure: remove the cooker from the stove and run cold water over it until the locking mechanism releases and the pressure subsides. Remove the lid and return the cooker to medium-high heat.

3 Cook, stirring constantly, until the rice is creamy and the sauce is thickened, about 1 minute.

Per serving (½ cup): 252 Cal, 1 g Fat, 0 g Sat Fat, 0 g Trans Fat, 2 mg Chol, 141 mg Sod, 54 g Carb, 1 g Fib, 8 g Prot, 171 mg Calc. *PointsPlus* value: **7.**

Oatmeal with Dried Fruit and Brown Sugar

SERVES 2

2 cups water

⅔ cup quick-cooking (not instant) oats

¼ cup dried cranberries

¼ cup dried peaches, halved and thinly sliced

2 dried figs, quartered

1 tablespoon packed brown sugar

½ teaspoon vanilla extract

½ teaspoon cinnamon

⅛ teaspoon salt

Bring the water to a boil in a medium saucepan over medium-high heat. Stir in the remaining ingredients and return to a boil. Reduce the heat to medium-low and simmer until the water is absorbed and the fruit is softened, about 8 minutes.

Per serving (about 1 cup): 278 Cal, 2 g Fat, 0 g Sat Fat, 0 g Trans Fat, 0 mg Chol, 153 mg Sod, 64 g Carb, 6 g Fib, 6 g Prot, 65 mg Calc. **PointsPlus** value: **7.**

⏱ Time-Saver

Use kitchen scissors to quickly cut dried fruit. To prevent the fruit from sticking to the blades, lightly spray them with nonstick spray.

Spiced Oatmeal Brûlée

SERVES 6

4 cups fat-free milk

¼ cup golden raisins

¼ cup dried blueberries

¼ cup dried cranberries

3 cups old-fashioned (rolled) oats

½ teaspoon cinnamon

¼ teaspoon nutmeg

¼ teaspoon salt

1½ tablespoons packed light brown sugar

1 Preheat the broiler.

2 Meanwhile, bring the milk to a low simmer in a large saucepan set over medium-high heat. Stir in all the remaining ingredients except the brown sugar. Cook, stirring frequently, about 2 minutes. Reduce the heat and simmer, stirring occasionally, until the oatmeal is creamy, about 3 minutes longer.

3 Spread the cereal mixture in an 8-inch square baking dish; sprinkle evenly with the brown sugar. Broil 5 inches from the heat until the sugar caramelizes, about 30 seconds. Let the oatmeal stand about 2 minutes before serving.

Per serving (½ cup): 277 Cal, 3 g Fat, 1 g Sat Fat, 0 g Trans Fat, 3 mg Chol, 187 mg Sod, 52 g Carb, 6 g Fib, 12 g Prot, 237 mg Calc. **PointsPlus** value: **7.**

Rich and Creamy Oatmeal with Blueberries and Walnuts

SERVES 4

3 cups water

2 cups quick-cooking (not instant) oats

¼ cup sugar

½ teaspoon cinnamon

½ cup fat-free milk

1½ cups thawed frozen fat-free whipped topping

1 cup fresh or thawed frozen blueberries

1 tablespoon chopped walnuts

1 Combine the water, oats, sugar, and cinnamon in a medium saucepan and bring to a boil. Cook, stirring constantly, until thickened, about 5 minutes.

2 Remove the saucepan from the heat and stir in the milk until combined. Fold in the whipped topping and blueberries; sprinkle with the walnuts.

Per serving (1 cup): 284 Cal, 4 g Fat, 1 g Sat Fat, 0 g Trans Fat, 1 mg Chol, 28 mg Sod, 56 g Carb, 5 g Fib, 8 g Prot, 74 mg Calc. *PointsPlus* value: **7.**

◆ Filling Extra

Double the amount of blueberries.

*Rich and Creamy Oatmeal
with Blueberries and Walnuts*

Fresh Fruit with Orange-Scented Ricotta

SERVES 4

6 cups mixed fruit (such as grapes, cubed melon, sliced strawberries, orange sections, and blackberries)

3 tablespoons chopped fresh mint

½ cup part-skim ricotta cheese

1 teaspoon grated orange zest

6 fresh mint sprigs (optional)

1 Combine the fruit and mint in a large bowl; divide evenly among 4 dishes.

2 Combine the ricotta and orange zest in a blender or food processor and puree. Spoon evenly over the fruit and garnish each serving with a mint sprig, if using.

Per serving (1 ½ cups fruit and about 2 tablespoons ricotta topping): 162 Cal, 3 g Fat, 2 g Sat Fat, 0 g Trans Fat, 9 mg Chol, 56 mg Sod, 30 g Carb, 5 g Fib, 6 g Prot, 114 mg Calc. *PointsPlus* value: **4.**

◆ Filling Extra

Enjoy a slice of toasted reduced-calorie whole wheat bread and get a dose of whole grains—a great start to your day! (1 slice toasted reduced-calorie whole wheat bread will increase the *PointsPlus* value by **1**.)

Mango-Honey Breakfast Cooler

SERVES 2

1 ripe mango, peeled,
   pitted, and cut into chunks
   (about 1 cup)

1 cup hulled and halved
   strawberries

1 kiwi fruit, peeled and cut into
   chunks

½ cup plain fat-free yogurt

2 tablespoons honey

1 teaspoon lime juice

6 ice cubes

2 strawberries

2 fresh mint sprigs

Combine the mango, strawberries, kiwi fruit, yogurt, honey, lime juice, and ice cubes in a blender and puree. Pour into 2 glasses and garnish each serving with a strawberry and a mint sprig.

Per serving (1 cup): 175 Cal, 1 g Fat, 0 g Sat Fat, 0 g Trans Fat, 1 mg Chol, 54 mg Sod, 41 g Carb, 5 g Fib, 5 g Prot, 162 mg Calc. *PointsPlus* value: **5.**

Mango-Peach Smoothie

SERVES 2

1 mango, peeled, pitted,
   and cut into chunks (about
   1 cup)

2 peaches, pitted and cut into
   chunks (1 cup)

½ cup plain fat-free yogurt

2 tablespoons honey

6 ice cubes

Combine all the ingredients in a blender and process until thick and smooth, about 2 minutes. Pour into 2 glasses.

Per serving (1 cup): 225 Cal, 1 g Fat, 0 g Sat Fat, 0 g Trans Fat, 1 mg, Chol, 54 mg Sod, 55 g Carb, 5 g Fib, 5 g Prot, 170 mg Calc. *PointsPlus* value: **6.**

Banana-Peach Protein Smoothie

SERVES 4

1 very ripe banana, peeled and cut into thirds

1 large peach, halved and pitted

5 large pitted dates

1 cup plain fat-free yogurt

⅔ cup unsweetened pineapple juice

¼ cup unflavored soy isolate protein powder

2 tablespoons toasted wheat germ

1½ cups ice cubes

Combine all the ingredients in a blender, in batches if necessary, and puree. Pour into 4 glasses.

Per serving (about 1 cup): 210 Cal, 1 g Fat, 0 g Sat Fat, 0 g Trans Fat, 1 mg Chol, 53 mg Sod, 44 g Carb, 5 g Fib, 10 g Prot, 157 mg Calc. *PointsPlus* value: **4.**

⏱ Time-Saver

Keep a stash of very ripe bananas in your freezer so you can make this smoothie at a moment's notice (you won't even need to thaw them).
To freeze bananas, peel them and transfer to a zip-close plastic freezer bag. Press out the air, seal the bag, and freeze up to 2 months.

Tropical Sorbet Smoothie

SERVES 2

1 cup strawberry sorbet, softened

½ cup canned crushed pineapple in juice, drained

½ cup orange juice

1 small banana, sliced

½ teaspoon vanilla extract

Combine all the ingredients in a blender and puree. Pour into 2 glasses.

Per serving (about 1 cup): 216 Cal, 0 g Fat, 0 g Sat Fat, 0 g Trans fat, 0 mg Chol, 32 mg Sod, 52 g Carb, 2 g Fib, 1 g Prot, 20 mg Calc. *PointsPlus* value: **6.**

Denver Omelette

SERVES 2

1 red bell pepper, chopped

⅓ cup chopped onion

¼ pound sliced lean deli ham, chopped

⅛ teaspoon black pepper

1 cup fat-free egg substitute

1 Spray a medium nonstick skillet with olive oil nonstick spray and set over medium heat. When a drop of water sizzles in it, add the bell pepper, onion, ham, and black pepper; cook, stirring occasionally, until the vegetables are softened, 4–5 minutes. Pour in the egg substitute and cook until almost set, about 3 minutes, gently lifting the edge of the eggs with a heatproof rubber spatula to allow the uncooked portion of egg to run underneath.

2 Fold the omelette in half and cook until set, about 2 minutes. Cut in half and place one portion on each of 2 plates.

Per serving (½ omelette): 182 Cal, 7 g Fat, 3 g Sat Fat, 0 g Trans Fat, 35 mg Chol, 946 mg Sod, 6 g Carb, 1 g Fib, 23 g Prot, 50 mg Calc. *PointsPlus* value: **4.**

⏱ Time-Saver

Keep a bag of frozen chopped onions in the freezer for times when you need only a small amount.

Provençal Vegetable Omelette

SERVES 2

1 cup halved grape tomatoes

1 small zucchini, thinly sliced

2 scallions, thinly sliced

¼ cup chopped fresh basil

¾ teaspoon herbes de Provence

½ teaspoon salt

¼ teaspoon black pepper

1 cup fat-free egg substitute

4 tablespoons shredded
  fat-free Swiss cheese

1 Lightly spray a medium nonstick skillet with olive oil nonstick spray and set over medium heat. Add the tomatoes, zucchini, scallions, herbes de Provence, salt, and pepper; cook, stirring, until the vegetables are slightly softened, about 3 minutes. Transfer to a bowl; set aside.

2 Wipe the skillet clean. Spray the skillet with nonstick spray and set over medium heat. When a drop of water sizzles in it, add ½ cup of the egg substitute and cook until almost set, about 3 minutes, gently lifting the edge of the eggs with a heatproof rubber spatula to allow the uncooked portion of egg to run underneath. Spoon half of the vegetable mixture over half of the omelette. Fold the unfilled portion of omelette over the filling and sprinkle with 2 tablespoons of the Swiss cheese. Slide the omelette onto a plate and keep warm. Repeat with the remaining egg substitute, vegetable mixture, and cheese to make another omelette.

Per serving (1 omelette): 152 Cal, 4 g Fat, 2 g Sat Fat, 0 g Trans Fat, 10 mg Chol, 1068 mg Sod, 11 g Carb, 3 g Fib, 19 g Prot, 418 mg Calc. *PointsPlus* value: **3.**

◆ Filling Extra

For a hearty side dish, toss 10 ounces cooked small potatoes with a mix of chopped fresh herbs and a bit of sea salt and black pepper. This will increase the per-serving *PointsPlus* value by **3.**

Potato and Green Pepper Frittata

SERVES 4

1 tablespoon olive oil

1 cup frozen hash-brown
potatoes

1 cup frozen chopped green bell
pepper

1 cup sliced white mushrooms

2 scallions, chopped

½ teaspoon dried oregano

¼ teaspoon salt

¼ teaspoon black pepper

3 large eggs

4 egg whites

2 tablespoons shredded cheddar
cheese

1 Heat the oil in a large nonstick skillet over medium-high heat. Add the potatoes, bell pepper, mushrooms, scallions, oregano, salt, and black pepper. Cook, stirring occasionally, until the vegetables are softened, about 6 minutes.

2 Meanwhile, lightly beat the eggs and egg whites in a medium bowl. Reduce the heat to medium; add the eggs and cook until almost set, about 3 minutes, lifting the edges frequently with a heatproof rubber spatula to allow the uncooked portion of egg to run underneath.

3 Sprinkle the cheddar evenly over the frittata. Reduce the heat to low and cook, covered, until the cheese melts slightly, about 3 minutes. Cut the frittata into 4 wedges.

Per serving (1 wedge): 175 Cal, 8 g Fat, 2 g Sat Fat, 0 g Trans Fat, 163 mg Chol, 443 mg Sod, 14 g Carb, 2 g Fib, 10 g Prot, 58 mg Calc. **PointsPlus** value: **4.**

⏱ Time-Saver

Purchase pre-sliced white mushrooms at the supermarket. For a deeper mushroom flavor, select sliced cremini mushrooms.

Crab and Chive Frittata

SERVES 4

1 red bell pepper, chopped

6 ounces fresh lump crabmeat, picked over

¼ cup chopped chives

½ teaspoon salt

¼ teaspoon black pepper

1½ cups fat-free egg substitute

⅔ cup fat-free ricotta cheese

1 Spray a large nonstick skillet with olive oil nonstick spray and set over medium-high heat. Add the bell pepper and cook, stirring, until softened, about 2 minutes. Add the crabmeat about 30 seconds. Pour the egg substitute evenly over the crab mixture and top with dollops of the ricotta.

2 Reduce the heat to low and cook, covered, until the eggs are set, about 8 minutes. Run a narrow spatula under the frittata to loosen it from the pan. Cut into 4 wedges.

Per serving (1 wedge): 157 Cal, 1 g Fat, 0 g Sat Fat, 0 g Trans Fat, 58 mg Chol, 663 mg Sod, 7 g Carb, 1 g Fib, 28 g Prot, 310 mg Calc. **PointsPlus** value: **3.**𝓟𝓟ᵛ

Time-Saver

Instead of spending time picking over the crabmeat for bits of shell and cartilage, prepare this elegant frittata with 1 (6-ounce) can crabmeat or drained tiny shrimp.

Crab and Chive Frittata

Southwestern-Style Scrambled Eggs

SERVES 4

4 (6-inch) corn tortillas

2 teaspoons canola oil

2 cups fat-free egg substitute

1 cup shredded reduced-fat cheddar cheese

1 (4-ounce) can chopped mild green chiles

2 tablespoons coarsely chopped fresh parsley

¼ teaspoon dried oregano

½ cup taco sauce, heated

1 Cut 1 tortilla in half and stack the halves; cut crosswise into 6 strips. Repeat with the remaining 3 tortillas to make a total of 48 strips.

2 Heat the oil in a large nonstick skillet over medium-high heat. Add the tortilla strips and cook, tossing frequently, until crisp and golden, about 5 minutes. Transfer to a plate; set aside.

3 Combine the egg substitute, cheddar, chiles, parsley, and oregano in a medium bowl.

4 Add to the skillet and cook, stirring occasionally, until the eggs are slightly set, about 2 minutes. Stir in the tortilla strips and cook, stirring, until the eggs are set, about 2 minutes longer. Serve with the taco sauce.

Per serving (¾ cup scrambled eggs and 2 tablespoons taco sauce): 243 Cal, 9 g Fat, 4 g Sat Fat, 0 g Trans Fat, 19 mg Chol, 734 mg Sod, 19 g Carb, 4 g Fib, 22 g Prot, 304 mg Calc. *PointsPlus* value: **5.**

⊙ Time-Saver

To heat the taco sauce quickly, microwave it in a microwavable glass measure on High 30 seconds.

Scrambled Eggs with Smoked Salmon and Onion

SERVES 4

2 teaspoons canola oil

1 large onion, thinly sliced

4 large eggs

6 egg whites

⅓ cup fat-free milk

¼ teaspoon black pepper

½-pound piece smoked salmon, chopped

½ cup fat-free sour cream

2 tablespoons chopped chives

1 Heat the oil in a large nonstick skillet over medium heat. Add the onion and cook, stirring, until softened, about 5 minutes.

2 Meanwhile, beat the eggs, egg whites, milk, and pepper in a large bowl. Pour evenly over the onion and cook, without stirring, 1 minute. Sprinkle the smoked salmon evenly over the eggs and cook, stirring frequently, until the eggs are set, about 4 minutes longer. Divide the eggs evenly among 4 plates. Top each serving with a dollop of the sour cream and ½ tablespoon of the chives.

Per serving (about 1 ⅓ cups eggs and 2 tablespoons sour cream): 235 Cal, 10 g Fat, 2 g Sat Fat, 0 g Trans Fat, 228 mg Chol, 642 mg Sod, 10 g Carb, 1 g Fib, 24 g Prot, 108 mg Calc. *PointsPlus* value: **6.**

Poached Eggs with Salsa and Cheese

SERVES 4

4 plum tomatoes, quartered

1 small red onion, quartered

½ jalapeño pepper, seeded
(wear gloves to prevent
irritation)

2 tablespoons coarsely chopped
fresh parsley

¼ teaspoon salt

1 teaspoon white vinegar

4 large eggs

4 (6-inch) fat-free corn tortillas,
warmed

4 tablespoons shredded
fat-free cheddar cheese

1 To make the salsa, put the tomatoes, onion, jalapeño, parsley, and salt in a food processor and pulse until coarsely chopped. Transfer to a small bowl; set aside.

2 Half-fill a large skillet with water and bring to a boil over high heat. Add the vinegar and reduce the heat so the water simmers slowly. Crack the eggs, one at a time, and lower into the skillet. Reduce the heat to a simmer and poach until the whites are set and the yolks are still runny, about 2 minutes. With a slotted spoon, transfer the eggs, one at a time, to a double thickness of paper towels to drain.

3 Place 1 tortilla on each of 4 plates and top with an egg. Sprinkle each egg with 1 tablespoon of the cheddar and top with one-fourth of the salsa.

Per serving (1 filled tortilla): 163 Cal, 6 g Fat, 2 g Sat Fat, 0 g Trans Fat, 213 mg Chol, 428 mg Sod, 17 g Carb, 2 g Fib, 10 g Prot, 140 mg Calc. ***PointsPlus*** value: **4.**

⏱ Time-Saver

Make a switch and use ¼ teaspoon hot pepper sauce instead of the jalapeño pepper.

Poached Eggs with Salsa and Cheese

Mixed Vegetable Egg Foo Yong

SERVES 4

3 large eggs

6 egg whites

1 teaspoon reduced-sodium soy sauce

¾ teaspoon salt

¼ teaspoon black pepper

2 teaspoons Asian (dark) sesame oil

1 onion, thinly sliced

6 shiitake mushrooms, stems discarded and caps sliced

½ cup packaged matchstick-cut carrots

1 celery stalk, thinly sliced

2 cups bean sprouts

1 Beat the eggs, egg whites, soy sauce, salt, and pepper in a medium bowl; set aside.

2 Spray a nonstick wok or large deep nonstick skillet with nonstick spray and set over medium-high heat. When a drop of water sizzles in it, add the sesame oil, tilting the pan to coat the bottom. Add the onion, mushrooms, carrots, and celery; stir-fry about 1 minute. Add the bean sprouts and stir-fry until the vegetables are crisp-tender, about 2 minutes. Add the egg mixture and stir-fry until set, 1–2 minutes longer.

Per serving (1 cup): 162 Cal, 9 g Fat, 2 g Sat Fat, 0 g Trans Fat, 159 mg Chol, 634 mg Sod, 7 g Carb, 2 g Fib, 16 g Prot, 65 mg Calc. **PointsPlus** value: **4.**

Time-Saver

If you can't find packaged matchstick-cut carrots at the supermarket, use an equal amount of broccoli slaw instead.

Apple-Raisin Matzo Brei

SERVES 4

4 (6-inch) squares whole-wheat matzo

2 cups boiling water

1 large apple, peeled, cored, and thinly sliced

¼ cup raisins

2 large eggs

1 egg white

¼ cup fat-free milk

1 tablespoon sugar

½ teaspoon orange zest

¼ teaspoon cinnamon

¼ teaspoon salt

1 Coarsely crumble the matzo into a large bowl; add the boiling water and let soak about 1 minute; drain off the water. Let cool about 5 minutes, then add the apple and raisins, stirring to combine.

2 Meanwhile, beat the eggs, egg white, milk, sugar, orange zest, cinnamon, and salt in a medium bowl. Pour over the matzo mixture, stirring to combine well.

3 Spray a large nonstick skillet with nonstick spray and set over medium heat. Add the matzo mixture, spreading it evenly. Cook, shaking the skillet occasionally, about 1 minute. Cook, covered, until firm and lightly browned on the bottom, about 4 minutes.

4 Uncover the skillet. Place a large plate on top and invert the skillet. Slide the matzo brei onto a large plate, then slide it back into the skillet and cook until set and lightly browned, about 1 minute longer. Cut into 4 wedges.

Per serving (1 wedge): 213 Cal, 4 g Fat, 1 g Sat Fat, 0 g Trans Fat, 106 mg Chol, 202 mg Sod, 39 g Carb, 4 g Fib, 8 g Prot, 52 mg Calc. *PointsPlus* value: **6.**

⏱ Time-Saver

Look for bags of sliced fresh apples in the produce section of the supermarket. You will need 2 cups for this recipe.

Smoked Salmon, Dill, and Red Onion Pizzas

SERVES 4

4 (10-inch) whole-wheat tortillas

⅔ cup reduced-fat sour cream

¼ cup prepared white
    horseradish

2 teaspoons grated lemon zest

½ teaspoon salt

¼ teaspoon black pepper

6 plum tomatoes, cut into
    ¼-inch dice

1 small red onion, thinly sliced

½ pound thinly sliced smoked
    salmon, cut crosswise into
    1½-inch-wide strips

2 tablespoons chopped
    fresh dill

1 Spray a large nonstick skillet with nonstick spray and set over medium-high heat. Add 1 tortilla and cook until crisp and golden, about 1½ minutes on each side. Transfer to a plate and keep warm. Repeat with the remaining tortillas.

2 Combine the sour cream, horseradish, lemon zest, salt, and pepper in a small bowl; spread evenly over each tortilla. Top evenly with the tomatoes, onion, smoked salmon, and dill.

Per serving (1 pizza): 288 Cal, 7 g Fat, 3 g Sat Fat, 0 g Trans Fat, 26 mg Chol, 1124 mg Sod, 40 g Carb, 7 g Fib, 19 g Prot, 97 mg Calc. *PointsPlus* value: **8.**

Smoked Salmon, Dill, and Red Onion Pizzas

Italian Salad Pizza

SERVES 6

1 (10-ounce) prebaked pizza crust

2 cups shredded romaine lettuce

1 tomato, seeded and chopped

1 small red onion, thinly sliced

2 carrots, shredded

1 cup peeled, seeded, and chopped cucumber

5 pitted kalamata olives, sliced

2 tablespoons balsamic vinegar

1½ tablespoons extra-virgin olive oil

½ teaspoon dried oregano

2 tablespoons grated Parmesan cheese

1 Place the pizza crust directly on an oven rack and turn the oven to 450°F. Bake 10 minutes.

2 Meanwhile, combine the lettuce, tomato, onion, carrots, cucumber, olives, vinegar, oil, and oregano in a large bowl. Top the pizza crust evenly with the salad mixture, leaving a ½-inch border. Sprinkle with the Parmesan and cut into 6 wedges.

Per serving (1 wedge): 212 Cal, 7 g Fat, 2 g Sat Fat, 0 g Trans Fat, 2 mg Chol, 360 mg Sod, 29 g Carb, 3 g Fib, 7 g Prot, 53 mg Calc. *PointsPlus* value: **5.**

Microwave Sausage and Chile Corn Bread

SERVES 6

1 ¼ cups all-purpose flour

¾ cup yellow cornmeal

2 teaspoons baking soda

½ teaspoon salt

¾ cup + 2 tablespoons
low-fat buttermilk

½ cup canned cream-style corn

¼ cup chopped red bell pepper

1 large egg

1 (4-ounce) can chopped mild or
hot green chiles

2 ounces ready-to-eat turkey
breakfast sausage, crumbled

1 Combine the flour, cornmeal, baking soda, and salt in a large bowl. Whisk together the buttermilk, corn, bell pepper, and egg in a medium bowl. Add the buttermilk mixture to the flour mixture and stir just until combined. Stir in the chiles and sausage.

2 Spray a 10-inch high-sided round microwavable dish with nonstick spray. Scrape the batter into the dish and spread evenly.

3 Microwave on High 4 minutes; cover with plastic wrap, venting one corner. Cook on High until firm and cooked through, 4–6 minutes longer. Let stand about 4 minutes, then cut into 6 wedges.

Per serving (1 wedge): 223 Cal, 3 g Fat, 1 g Sat Fat, 0 g Trans Fat, 42 mg Chol, 834 mg Sod, 40 g Carb, 2 g Fib, 9 g Prot, 59 mg Calc. **PointsPlus** value: **6.**

Turkey, Potato, and Sage Patties

SERVES 4

2 baking potatoes, peeled

1 large onion, peeled

1 pound ground skinless turkey breast

2 egg whites

2 tablespoons Worcestershire sauce

2 teaspoons dried sage

1 teaspoon salt

½ teaspoon black pepper

4 teaspoons canola oil

1 Grate the potato and onion into a large bowl. Add the turkey, egg whites, Worcestershire sauce, sage, salt, and pepper; mix until well combined. With damp hands, form the mixture into 16 patties.

2 Heat 2 teaspoons of the oil in a large nonstick skillet over medium-high heat. Add the patties, in batches, and cook until browned and cooked through, about 4 minutes on each side.

Per serving (4 patties): 190 Cal, 4 g Fat, 0 g Sat Fat, 0 g Trans Fat, 40 mg Chol, 696 mg Sod, 16 g Carb, 2 g Fib, 20 g Prot, 32 mg Calc. **PointsPlus** value: **6.**

◆ Filling Extra

These savory patties are excellent with hard-cooked eggs (1 hard-cooked large egg per serving will increase the **PointsPlus** value by **2**).

Pinto Bean and Pepper Jack Burritos

SERVES 4

1 cup canned pinto beans, rinsed and drained

1½ teaspoons chili powder

2 teaspoons ground cumin

1 cup fat-free egg substitute

4 (10-inch) fat-free whole-wheat tortillas, warmed

4 tablespoons shredded reduced-fat pepper Jack cheese

4 tablespoons prepared salsa

1 Spray a medium nonstick skillet with nonstick spray and set over medium-high heat. Add the pinto beans, chili powder, and cumin; cook, stirring, until heated through, about 5 minutes. Add the egg substitute and cook, stirring, until set, about 3 minutes.

2 Place one-fourth of the egg mixture along one side of each tortilla and top with 1 tablespoon of the pepper Jack and 1 tablespoon of the salsa. Roll the tortillas up to enclose the filling.

Per serving (1 burrito): 342 Cal, 3 g Fat, 1 g Sat Fat, 0 g Trans Fat, 5 mg Chol, 1203 mg Sod, 59 g Carb, 11 g Fib, 24 g Prot, 207 mg Calc. *PointsPlus* value: **6.**

⏱ Time-Saver

Use 2 teaspoons taco or Mexican seasoning and omit the chili powder and cumin.

Roast Beef and
Watercress Sandwiches

2

It's Noon . . . Time to Eat

Pork, Orange, and Fennel Salad

Bartlett Pear and Ham Salad

Frisée Salad with Canadian Bacon and Poached Eggs

Lebanese Chicken-Pita Salad

Santa Fe—Style Roasted Chicken Salad

Easy Salmon Niçoise

Tuna Salad—Stuffed Tomatoes

Shrimp and Papaya Salad with Honey-Lime Dressing

Asparagus-Shrimp Salad

Citrus and Scallop Salad

Chickpea and Feta Cheese Salad

Roast Beef and Watercress Sandwiches

Buffalo-Style Chicken Strips

Open-Face Chicken, Tomato, and Arugula Panini

Warm Caesar-Style Chicken Sandwiches

Turkey, Apple, and Honey-Mustard Wraps

Soy-Glazed Fresh Tuna Sandwiches

Salmon Salad Sandwiches

Asian-Style Shrimp Salad Sandwiches

Grilled Vegetable—Gruyère Sandwiches

Avocado, Tofu, and Tomato Sandwiches

Faux Egg Salad Sandwiches

Microwave Potato Nachos

Broccoli and Cheddar Quesadillas

White Bean and Roasted Pepper Bruschetta

Barley Soup with Chicken and Vegetables

Kielbasa and Black Bean Soup

Pea Soup with Shrimp and Tarragon

Corn and Crab Chowder

Tomato-Basil Soup

Easy Garden Vegetable Soup

Double Mushroom Broth with Soba Noodles

Pork, Orange, and Fennel Salad

SERVES 4

2 tablespoons red-wine vinegar

2 teaspoons olive oil

½ teaspoon salt

1 head frisée lettuce, torn into bite-size pieces

2 oranges, peeled and sectioned

1 small fennel bulb, trimmed and thinly sliced

1 red onion, thinly sliced

8 pitted kalamata olives, halved

¾ pound thinly sliced trimmed roasted pork loin

1 Whisk together the vinegar, oil, and salt in a small bowl; set aside.

2 Combine all the remaining ingredients except the pork in a large bowl. Drizzle with the dressing and gently toss to combine. Divide the salad evenly among 4 plates and top evenly with the pork.

Per serving (¼ of salad): 277 Cal, 12 g Fat, 3 g Sat Fat, 0 g Trans Fat, 71 mg Chol, 449 mg Sod, 16 g Carb, 5 g Fib, 27 g Prot, 95 mg Calc. **PointsPlus** value: **6.**

⏱ Time-Saver

Instead of taking the time to peel and section the oranges, use 2 cups drained refrigerated fresh citrus salad sections of red and white grapefruits and oranges. You'll find citrus salad in jars in the produce section of the supermarket.

*Pork, Orange,
and Fennel Salad*

Bartlett Pear and Ham Salad

SERVES 6

3 tablespoons champagne
   vinegar

2 tablespoons orange juice

1 tablespoon honey

1 tablespoon olive oil

1 teaspoon Dijon mustard

⅛ teaspoon salt

¼ teaspoon black pepper

2 firm-ripe Bartlett pears, halved,
   cored, and thinly sliced

1 McIntosh apple, halved, cored,
   and thinly sliced

1 (1-pound) piece fat-free honey-
   baked ham, cut into ½-inch
   pieces

4 cups hearts of romaine lettuce
   leaves, torn if large

Whisk together the vinegar, orange juice, honey, oil, mustard, salt, and pepper in a serving bowl. Add the remaining ingredients and toss to coat evenly.

Per serving (about 1 ½ cups): 143 Cal, 4 g Fat, 1 g Sat Fat, 0 g Trans Fat, 24 mg Chol, 966 mg Sod, 19 g Carb, 3 g Fib, 9 g Prot, 21 mg Calc. *PointsPlus* value: **5.**

Frisée Salad with Canadian Bacon and Poached Eggs

SERVES 4

½ pound sliced Canadian bacon, cut into strips

8 cups lightly packed torn frisée lettuce

2 tablespoons + 2 teaspoons apple-cider vinegar

4 large eggs

1 tablespoon olive oil

2 shallots, finely chopped

¼ cup reduced-sodium chicken broth

2 teaspoons Dijon mustard

¼ teaspoon salt

⅛ teaspoon black pepper

1 Half-fill a large skillet with water; bring to a boil.

2 Meanwhile, spray a large nonstick skillet with nonstick spray and set over medium heat. Add the bacon; cook, stirring, until browned, about 4 minutes. Transfer to paper towels to drain. Put the bacon into a large bowl and add the frisée.

3 When the water comes to a boil add 2 teaspoons of the vinegar. Crack the eggs, one at a time, and lower into the skillet. Reduce the heat to a simmer and poach until the whites are set and the yolks are still runny, about 2 minutes. With a slotted spoon, transfer the eggs, one at a time, to a double thickness of paper towels to drain.

4 Add the oil to the bacon skillet and set over medium heat. Add the shallots; cook until softened, about 2 minutes. Add the broth and bring to a simmer, scraping up any browned bits from the bottom of the pan. Boil until the pan liquid is reduced to a glaze, about 20 seconds. Stir in the remaining 2 tablespoons vinegar, the mustard, salt, and pepper. Pour over the greens and bacon; toss to coat evenly. Divide the salad evenly among 4 plates and top each salad with a poached egg.

Per serving (2 cups dressed greens and 1 egg): 220 Cal, 13 g Fat, 3 g Sat Fat, 0 g Trans Fat, 239 mg Chol, 1055 mg Sod, 6 g Carb, 3 g Fib, 20 g Prot, 100 mg Calc. *PointsPlus* value: **5**.

⊙ Time-Saver

Slice 4 hard-cooked eggs purchased from a supermarket salad bar and use them instead of making the poached eggs.

Lebanese Chicken-Pita Salad

SERVES 4

1 pound thin-sliced chicken breast, cut into bite-size pieces

½ teaspoon salt

¼ teaspoon black pepper

3 (6-inch) whole-wheat pita breads, toasted

12 cherry tomatoes, halved

1 cucumber, peeled, halved, seeded, and chopped

2 scallions, sliced

¼ cup lightly packed chopped fresh mint

¼ cup lightly packed chopped fresh cilantro

3 tablespoons lemon juice

2 teaspoons olive oil

1 teaspoon ground cumin

1 Sprinkle the chicken with ¼ teaspoon of the salt and ⅛ teaspoon of the pepper. Spray a large nonstick skillet with nonstick spray and set over medium-high heat. Add the chicken and cook, stirring, until cooked through, about 5 minutes; transfer to a serving bowl. Set aside.

2 Tear the pitas into 1-inch pieces and add to the bowl along with the tomatoes, cucumber, scallions, mint, cilantro, lemon juice, oil, cumin, and the remaining ¼ teaspoon salt and ⅛ teaspoon pepper. Toss to mix well.

Per serving (about 2 cups): 292 Cal, 7 g Fat, 2 g Sat Fat, 0 g Trans Fat, 68 mg Chol, 583 mg Sod, 27 g Carb, 4 g Fib, 30 g Prot, 47 mg Calc. *PointsPlus* value: **7.**

⏱ Time-Saver

Instead of cooking the chicken in step 1, use a 10-ounce package of sliced grilled chicken breast.

Lebanese Chicken-Pita Salad

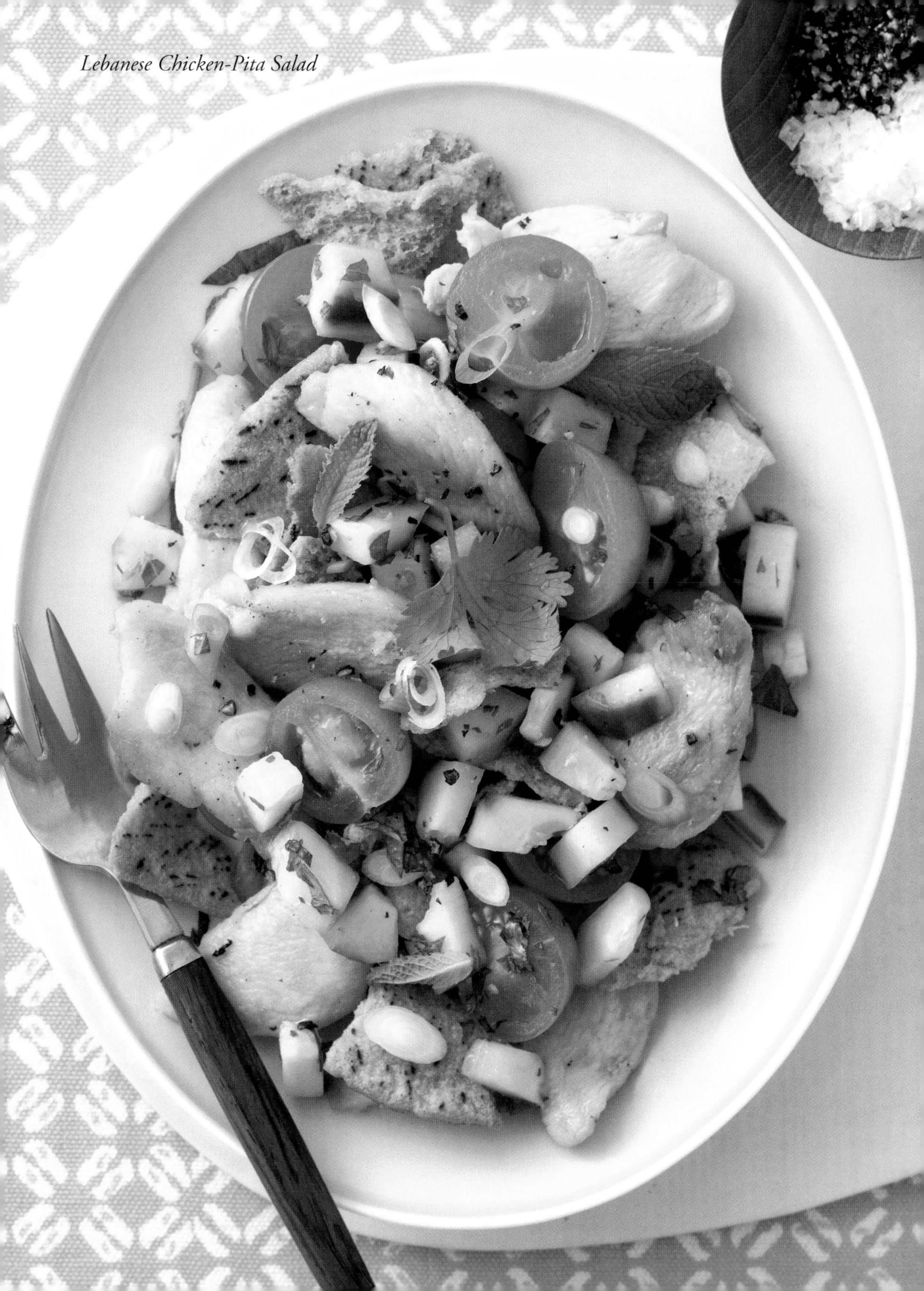

Santa Fe—Style Roasted Chicken Salad

SERVES 6

3 tablespoons lime juice

2 tablespoons taco sauce

2 tablespoons olive oil

2 tablespoons sliced pickled jalapeño pepper, drained and chopped

1 teaspoon ground cumin

¾ teaspoon salt

3 cups sliced deli roast chicken breast

3 cups mixed baby salad greens

1 cup halved grape tomatoes

4 scallions, chopped

½ cup chopped fresh cilantro

Whisk together the lime juice, taco sauce, oil, jalapeño, cumin, and salt in a serving bowl. Add the remaining ingredients and gently toss to coat evenly.

Per serving (generous 1 cup): 175 Cal, 7 g Fat, 1 g Sat Fat, 0 g Trans Fat, 60 mg Chol, 391 mg Sod, 4 g Carb, 1 g Fib, 23 g Prot, 61 mg Calc. *PointsPlus* value: **4.**

Easy Salmon Niçoise

SERVES 2

Boston lettuce leaves

1 (7½-ounce) can red salmon,
  drained and flaked

4 cups assorted salad
  bar–type vegetables,
  such as cooked green beans,
  cherry tomatoes, baby carrots,
  sliced mushrooms, sliced red
  bell pepper, broccoli florets,
  and sliced red onion

6 niçoise olives

⅓ cup fat-free Italian dressing

Line a platter with the lettuce leaves. Mound the salmon in the center and arrange the vegetables in piles around the salmon. Scatter the olives over the vegetables and drizzle with the dressing.

Per serving (about 2 ½ cups salad): 223 Cal, 7 g Fat, 1 g Sat Fat, 0 g Trans Fat, 73 mg Chol, 1125 mg Sod, 20 g Carb, 6 g Fib, 25 g Prot, 325 mg Calc. **PointsPlus** value: **6.**

Tuna Salad—Stuffed Tomatoes

SERVES 4

4 large tomatoes

2 celery stalks

1 small carrot

2 shallots

2 (6-ounce) cans water-packed tuna, drained and flaked

¼ cup lemon juice

¼ cup reduced-fat mayonnaise

½ teaspoon black pepper

1 Slice off and discard the top third of each tomato. With a small spoon, scoop out and discard the seeds and inner flesh; set the tomatoes aside.

2 Combine the celery, carrot, and shallots in a food processor; pulse until chopped. Add the tuna and process until mixed well. Add the remaining ingredients and pulse just until combined. Fill the tomatoes evenly with the tuna mixture.

Per serving (1 stuffed tomato): 178 Cal, 6 g Fat, 1 g Sat Fat, 0 g Trans Fat, 28 mg Chol, 410 mg Sod, 11 g Carb, 2 g Fib, 21 g Prot, 41 mg Calc. **PointsPlus** value: **4.**

⏱ Time-Saver

If you prefer not to fuss making tomato shells, cut the tomatoes into thick slices, arrange on a platter, and top with the tuna salad.

Shrimp and Papaya Salad with Honey-Lime Dressing

SERVES 4

1 teaspoon grated orange zest

3 tablespoons orange juice

2 tablespoons lemon juice

1 tablespoon honey

1 teaspoon olive oil

¼ teaspoon salt

¼ teaspoon black pepper

Pinch cayenne

1 pound peeled and deveined cooked large shrimp

2 ripe papayas, peeled, halved, seeded, and cut into ¾-inch chunks

½ red bell pepper, thinly sliced

¼ cup lightly packed chopped fresh mint

4 cups mixed baby salad greens

1   Whisk together the orange zest and juice, lemon juice, honey, oil, salt, black pepper, and cayenne in a large bowl.

2   Add the shrimp, papayas, bell pepper, and mint; toss to coat evenly. Pile the salad greens on a platter and top with the shrimp-papaya mixture.

Per serving (about 2 cups): 223 Cal, 3 g Fat, 1 g Sat Fat, 0 g Trans Fat, 221 mg Chol, 434 mg Sod, 25 g Carb, 3 g Fib, 25 g Prot, 100 mg Calc. **PointsPlus** value: **6.**

Asparagus-Shrimp Salad

SERVES 4

1 pound asparagus, trimmed and cut into 2-inch lengths

2 tablespoons lemon juice

1½ tablespoons olive oil

½ teaspoon salt

¼ teaspoon black pepper

1 pound peeled and deveined cooked medium shrimp

1 cup halved grape tomatoes

½ small red onion, thinly sliced

2 tablespoons chopped fresh parsley

2 hard-cooked eggs, sliced

1 Fill a large skillet with 1 inch of water and bring to a boil over high heat. Add the asparagus and cook, covered, until crisp-tender, about 5 minutes; drain and rinse under cool running water.

2 Meanwhile, whisk together the lemon juice, oil, salt, and pepper in a small bowl; set aside.

3 Transfer the asparagus to a large bowl. Add the shrimp, tomatoes, onion, and parsley. Drizzle with the dressing and toss to coat evenly. Top with the eggs.

Per serving (about 1 ½ cups): 225 Cal, 9 g Fat, 2 g Sat Fat, 0 g Trans Fat, 327 mg Chol, 586 mg Sod, 6 g Carb, 2 g Fib, 29 g Prot, 82 mg Calc. **PointsPlus** value: **6.**

Time-Saver

Pick up hard-cooked eggs from a supermarket salad bar.

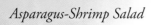
Asparagus-Shrimp Salad

Citrus and Scallop Salad

SERVES 4

1 pound sea scallops

¾ teaspoon salt

¼ teaspoon black pepper

¼ cup orange juice

2 tablespoons olive oil

1 tablespoon lemon juice

2 navel oranges, peeled and sectioned

1 ruby red grapefruit, peeled and sectioned

⅓ English (seedless) cucumber, halved lengthwise and sliced

3 scallions, sliced on the diagonal

6 pitted black olives, chopped

4 cups lightly packed baby arugula

1 Sprinkle the scallops with ½ teaspoon of the salt and the pepper. Spray a large nonstick skillet with nonstick spray and set over medium-high heat. Add the scallops to the skillet and cook until browned and just opaque throughout, about 2 minutes on each side.

2 Meanwhile, whisk together the orange juice, oil, lemon juice, and the remaining ¼ teaspoon salt in a large bowl. Add the oranges, grapefruit, cucumber, scallions, and olives; toss to coat evenly with the dressing. Add the scallops and gently toss to combine. Divide the arugula evenly among 4 plates; top evenly with the salad.

Per serving (about 2 ½ cups): 251 Cal, 9 g Fat, 1 g Sat Fat, 0 g Trans Fat, 37 mg Chol, 677 mg Sod, 23 g Carb, 4 g Fib, 21 g Prot, 99 mg Calc. *PointsPlus* value: **6.**

Chickpea and Feta Cheese Salad

SERVES 4

1 teaspoon grated lemon zest

2 tablespoons lemon juice

1 teaspoon olive oil

1 garlic clove, minced

¼ teaspoon salt

1 (15-ounce) can chickpeas, rinsed and drained

1 tomato, chopped

2 scallions, sliced

3 tablespoons chopped fresh parsley

3 cups lightly packed herb salad mix

2 ounces reduced-fat feta cheese, crumbled

Whisk together the lemon zest and juice, oil, garlic, and salt in a serving bowl. Add the chickpeas, tomato, scallions, parsley, and salad mix; toss to coat evenly with the dressing. Sprinkle with the feta.

Per serving (generous 1 cup): 178 Cal, 5 g Fat, 1 g Sat Fat, 0 g Trans Fat, 5 mg Chol, 453 mg Sod, 26 g Carb, 6 g Fib, 10 g Prot, 131 mg Calc. **PointsPlus** value: **4.**

◆ Filling Extra

If you like, spoon each portion of this salad over ½ cup cooked whole wheat couscous. This will increase the per-serving **PointsPlus** value by **3.**

Roast Beef and Watercress Sandwiches

SERVES 4

3 tablespoons light sour cream

1 tablespoon prepared horseradish, drained

1 tablespoon spicy brown mustard

⅛ teaspoon salt

⅛ teaspoon black pepper

2 cups lightly packed trimmed watercress

8 slices high-fiber bread

½ pound very thinly sliced deli roast beef

1 large tomato, thinly sliced

1 Combine the sour cream, horseradish, mustard, salt, and pepper in a small bowl; set aside.

2 Place the watercress on 4 slices of the bread. Top evenly with the roast beef and tomato. Spread the horseradish mixture evenly on the remaining 4 slices of bread; cover the sandwiches with the bread. Cut the sandwiches in half.

Per serving (1 sandwich): 207 Cal, 5 g Fat, 2 g Sat Fat, 0 g Trans Fat, 32 mg Chol, 1008 mg Sod, 29 g Carb, 8 g Fib, 18 g Prot, 88 mg Calc. *PointsPlus* value: **6.**

Roast Beef and
Watercress Sandwiches

Buffalo-Style Chicken Strips

SERVES 4

1 teaspoon hot pepper sauce

¼ cup Louisiana-style hot sauce

1 teaspoon Worcestershire sauce

1 tablespoon unsalted butter

1 pound skinless boneless
chicken breast halves, cut on
the diagonal into 1-inch-wide
strips

3 carrots, cut into ¼-inch
matchsticks

4 celery stalks, cut into
¼-inch matchsticks

½ cup fat-free blue cheese
dressing

1 Combine the pepper sauce, hot sauce, and Worcestershire sauce in a small saucepan and set over medium heat. Bring to a boil; reduce the heat and simmer 1 minute. Remove from the heat and add 1 teaspoon of the butter, stirring until melted.

2 Melt the remaining 2 teaspoons butter in a large nonstick skillet over medium heat. Add the chicken and cook, stirring, until browned and cooked through, 8–10 minutes. Add the hot-sauce mixture and cook, tossing, about 1 minute longer. Transfer the chicken to a serving bowl and serve with the carrots, celery, and blue cheese dressing.

Per serving (1 chicken breast half, about ⅓ cup carrot sticks, about ½ cup celery sticks, and 2 tablespoons dressing): 231 Cal, 7 g Fat, 3 g Sat Fat, 0 g Trans Fat, 77 mg Chol, 805 mg Sod, 15 g Carb, 3 g Fib, 26 g Prot, 71 mg Calc. *PointsPlus* value: **5.**

Open-Face Chicken, Tomato, and Arugula Panini

SERVES 4

4 (5-ounce) skinless boneless chicken breast halves

¼ teaspoon salt

⅛ teaspoon black pepper

4 teaspoons olive oil

2 tablespoons finely chopped fresh rosemary

1 tablespoon coarse-grained Dijon mustard

2 (4-ounce) ciabatta rolls, split

½ cup lightly packed baby arugula

1 large tomato, sliced

1 Sprinkle the chicken with the salt and pepper. Heat 2 teaspoons of the oil in a large nonstick skillet over medium-high heat. Add the chicken and cook until browned and cooked through, about 4 minutes on each side. Transfer to a plate.

2 Meanwhile, combine the rosemary and mustard in a cup. Slowly whisk in the remaining 2 teaspoons oil. Brush the cut sides of the rolls with the rosemary-mustard mixture. Place a chicken breast half on each roll half and top evenly with the tomato and arugula.

Per serving (1 sandwich): 359 Cal, 11 g Fat, 2 g Sat Fat, 0 g Trans Fat, 68 mg Chol, 614 mg Sod, 32 g Carb, 2 g Fib, 31 g Prot, 80 mg Calc. **PointsPlus** value: **9.**

◆ Filling Extra

Cut 2 carrots and 2 celery stalks into thick matchsticks to serve alongside the panini.

Warm Caesar-Style Chicken Sandwiches

SERVES 4

1 pound chicken tenders

¼ teaspoon black pepper

4 (2-ounce) whole-wheat rolls, split

¼ cup low-fat Caesar dressing

3 tablespoons coarsely grated Parmesan cheese

4 romaine lettuce leaves

1 Spray a large nonstick skillet with nonstick spray and set over medium-high heat. Sprinkle the chicken with the pepper and add to the skillet. Cook the chicken until lightly browned and cooked through, about 3 minutes on each side. Transfer to a plate; set aside.

2 Put the rolls, cut side down, in the skillet and toast until golden, about 2 minutes. Put one-fourth of the chicken on the bottom half of each roll. Drizzle evenly with the dressing and sprinkle with the Parmesan. Top each sandwich with a romaine leaf and cover with the tops of the rolls.

Per serving (1 sandwich): 322 Cal, 8 g Fat, 2 g Sat Fat, 0 g Trans Fat, 72 mg Chol, 578 mg Sod, 27 g Carb, 4 g Fib, 35 g Prot, 149 mg Calc. **PointsPlus** value: **8.**

Turkey, Apple, and Honey-Mustard Wraps

SERVES 4

¼ cup honey mustard

4 (8-inch) reduced-fat flour
tortillas

4 red leaf lettuce leaves

½ pound thinly sliced deli maple
turkey breast

¼ pound thinly sliced reduced-
fat Jarlsberg cheese

1 Golden Delicious apple,
peeled, cored, and thinly
sliced

Spread 1 tablespoon of the honey mustard on each tortilla. Top evenly with the lettuce, turkey, Jarlsberg, and apple. Fold in two opposite sides of each tortilla to form a cone.

Per serving (1 wrap): 362 Cal, 9 g Fat, 3 g Sat Fat, 0 g Trans Fat, 62 mg Chol, 716 mg Sod, 43 g Carb, 11 g Fib, 30 g Prot, 349 mg Calc. **PointsPlus** value: **8.**

Soy-Glazed Fresh Tuna Sandwiches

SERVES 4

4 tablespoons reduced-sodium soy sauce

2 tablespoons unseasoned rice vinegar

1 tablespoon honey

4 (5-ounce) tuna steaks

2 tablespoons reduced-fat mayonnaise

1 teaspoon Asian (dark) sesame oil

8 slices country-style bread

1 cup pea or alfalfa sprouts

2 scallions, thinly sliced

1 Combine 3 tablespoons of the soy sauce, the vinegar, and honey in a large shallow bowl or pie plate. Add the tuna, turning to coat; let stand about 5 minutes.

2 Meanwhile, combine the mayonnaise, sesame oil, and the remaining 1 tablespoon soy sauce in a cup.

3 Spray a large nonstick grill pan or skillet with nonstick spray and set over medium-high heat. Add the tuna and cook until pink in the center, 3–4 minutes on each side.

4 Spread the mayonnaise mixture evenly on 4 slices of the bread. Top evenly with the sprouts and scallions. Place a tuna steak on each and cover with the remaining slices of bread.

Per serving (1 sandwich): 380 Cal, 10 g Fat, 2 g Sat Fat, 0 g Trans Fat, 66 mg Chol, 913 mg Sod, 37 g Carb, 7 g Fib, 35 g Prot, 107 mg Calc. *PointsPlus* value: **11.**

Soy-Glazed Fresh Tuna Sandwiches

Salmon Salad Sandwiches

SERVES 4

1 (14¾-ounce) can salmon,
drained and flaked

3 tablespoons reduced-fat
mayonnaise

2 tablespoons chopped pickle

1 tablespoon prepared
horseradish

2 teaspoons grated lemon zest

2 teaspoons Dijon mustard

2 cups lightly packed trimmed
watercress

4 (4-ounce) whole-wheat rolls,
split

4 thick tomato slices

1 Toss together the salmon, mayonnaise, pickle, horseradish, lemon zest, and mustard in a medium bowl.

2 Divide the watercress among the bottom halves of the rolls. Top each with 1 tomato slice and ½ cup of the salmon salad. Cover with the tops of the rolls.

Per serving (1 sandwich): 306 Cal, 12 g Fat, 2 g Sat Fat, 1 g Trans Fat, 18 mg Chol, 865 mg Sod, 32 g Carb, 4 g Fib, 19 g Prot, 259 mg Calc. **PointsPlus** value: **8.**

◆ *Filling Extra*

Serve the sandwiches with a simple side salad of thinly sliced English (seedless) cucumber and thinly sliced radishes tossed with a touch of unseasoned rice vinegar.

Asian-Style Shrimp Salad Sandwiches

SERVES 4

- 3 tablespoons lime juice
- 2 tablespoons chopped fresh cilantro
- 2 tablespoons chopped fresh mint
- 1 tablespoon Asian fish sauce
- 2 teaspoons sugar
- ¾ pound frozen cooked baby shrimp, thawed
- ½ cup packaged matchstick-cut carrots
- ½ small yellow bell pepper, chopped
- 1 shallot, finely chopped
- 4 (6-inch) pita breads
- 4 Boston lettuce leaves

1 Combine the lime juice, cilantro, mint, fish sauce, and sugar in a large bowl. Add the shrimp, carrots, bell pepper, and shallot; toss to combine.

2 Cut off and discard the top third of each pita. Line each pita with a lettuce leaf; fill evenly with the shrimp mixture.

Per serving (1 sandwich): 234 Cal, 2 g Fat, 0 g Sat Fat, 0 g Trans Fat, 166 mg Chol, 783 mg Sod, 31 g Carb, 2 g Fib, 23 g Prot, 92 mg Calc. **PointsPlus** value: **6.**

 *Filling Extra*

Round out the meal with a salad of baby spinach tossed with a splash of seasoned rice vinegar.

Grilled Vegetable—Gruyère Sandwiches

SERVES 4

1 (¾-pound) eggplant, cut into ¼-inch rounds

2 zucchini, cut on the diagonal into ¼-inch slices

¾ teaspoon salt

½ teaspoon black pepper

¼ cup-reduced-fat mayonnaise

2 teaspoons chopped fresh thyme

1 garlic clove, crushed through a press

8 thin slices sourdough bread, lightly toasted

1 cup lightly packed baby arugula

½ cup drained roasted red pepper cut into strips

4 tablespoons shredded Gruyère cheese

1 Spray the rack of a broiler with nonstick spray and preheat the broiler.

2 Spray the eggplant and zucchini with nonstick spray; sprinkle with the salt and pepper. Arrange on the broiler rack and broil 4 inches from the heat until tender and lightly browned, about 4 minutes on each side.

3 Meanwhile, combine the mayonnaise, thyme, and garlic in a small bowl. Spread the mixture on 4 slices of the toasted bread. Layer the eggplant and zucchini evenly on the bread and top each with ¼ cup of the arugula, one-fourth of the roasted pepper, and 1 tablespoon of the Gruyère. Cover the sandwiches with the remaining slices of toast. Cut each sandwich in half on the diagonal.

Per serving (1 sandwich): 294 Cal, 9 g Fat, 3 g Sat Fat, 0 g Trans Fat, 12 mg Chol, 1,007 mg Sod, 44 g Carb, 4 g Fib, 11 g Prot, 127 mg Calc. **PointsPlus** value: **7.**

Avocado, Tofu, and Tomato Sandwiches

SERVES 4

¼ cup fat-free mayonnaise

8 slices whole-grain bread, toasted

½ avocado, halved, pitted, peeled, and thinly sliced

12 ounces firm tofu, thinly sliced

1 large tomato, thinly sliced

1 large carrot, shredded

½ teaspoon salt

½ teaspoon black pepper

1 bunch watercress, trimmed

Spread the mayonnaise evenly on 4 slices of the bread. Layer evenly with the avocado, tofu, tomato, and carrot. Sprinkle with the salt and pepper and top evenly with the watercress. Cover with the remaining slices of toast and cut the sandwiches in half.

Per serving (1 sandwich): 278 Cal, 10 g Fat, 2 g Sat Fat, 0 g Trans Fat, 2 mg Chol, 723 mg Sod, 33 g Carb, 8 g Fib, 18 g Prot, 334 mg Calc. **PointsPlus** value: **7.**

⏱ Time-Saver

To prep the avocado in a flash, cut it lengthwise around the seed and rotate the halves to separate. Slide the tip of a spoon gently underneath the seed and lift it out, then scoop out the avocado flesh with the spoon.

Pea Soup with Shrimp and Tarragon

SERVES 4

1 tablespoon unsalted butter

2 onions, chopped

1 (10-ounce) package frozen peas

1¾ cups reduced-sodium chicken broth

1 cup low-fat buttermilk

1 tablespoon fresh tarragon leaves

¼ teaspoon salt

⅛ teaspoon black pepper

½ pound peeled and deveined cooked medium shrimp

4 fresh tarragon sprigs

2 very thin lemon slices, halved (optional)

1 Melt the butter in a large saucepan over medium heat. Add the onions and cook, stirring, until softened, about 4 minutes. Stir in the peas and broth; bring to a boil. Reduce the heat and simmer about 5 minutes. Remove the saucepan from the heat; stir in the buttermilk, tarragon, salt, and pepper; let cool about 5 minutes.

2 Transfer the soup to a blender or food processor, in batches if necessary, and puree. Ladle evenly into 4 bowls and top evenly with the shrimp. Garnish each serving with a tarragon sprig and a lemon slice, if using.

Per serving (1 cup): 197 Cal, 5 g Fat, 2 g Sat Fat, 0 g Trans Fat, 67 mg Chol, 728 mg Sod, 18 g Carb, 4 g Fib, 20 g Prot, 157 mg Calc. *PointsPlus* value: **5.**

Time-Saver

Skip the hassle of chopping fresh onions—and the tears—by using 2 cups of always-convenient frozen chopped onion.

Corn and Crab Chowder

SERVES 4

1 tablespoon canola oil

2 (10-ounce) packages frozen
corn kernels, thawed

1 onion, chopped

2 (8-ounce) bottles clam juice

1 (14½-ounce) can reduced-
sodium chicken broth

½ teaspoon dried thyme

½ teaspoon salt

¼ teaspoon black pepper

¼ teaspoon cayenne

¾ pound lump crabmeat, picked
over

1 Heat the oil in a large saucepan over medium-high heat. Add the corn and onion; cook, stirring occasionally, until softened, about 6 minutes.

2 Add the clam juice, broth, thyme, salt, pepper, and cayenne; cover and bring to a boil. Reduce the heat and simmer about 5 minutes. Remove the saucepan from the heat and let cool about 5 minutes.

3 Transfer the soup to a blender, in batches if necessary, and puree. Return the soup to the saucepan; stir in the crabmeat and cook over medium heat until heated through, about 2 minutes.

Per serving (generous 1½ cups): 243 Cal, 6 g Fat, 0 g Sat Fat, 0 g Trans Fat, 83 mg Chol, 999 mg Sod, 30 g Carb, 5 g Fib, 21 g Prot, 119 mg Calc. **PointsPlus** value: **7.**

⏱ Time-Saver

To save on your prep time, use 2 (6-ounce) cans of lump crabmeat. It will not need to be picked over for bits of cartilage.

Tomato-Basil Soup

SERVES 6

2 all-purpose potatoes, scrubbed and cut into ½-inch dice

1 onion, chopped

1 cup packaged matchstick-cut carrots

6 cups reduced-sodium chicken broth

2 zucchini, quartered lengthwise and sliced

1 (14½-ounce) can diced tomatoes, drained

1 cup frozen cut green beans

1 cup frozen peas

¼ teaspoon black pepper

¼ cup lightly packed torn fresh basil

¼ cup shredded fat-free Swiss cheese

Combine the potatoes, onion, carrots, and broth in a large saucepan; bring to a boil over medium-high heat. Reduce the heat and simmer, covered, about 5 minutes. Stir in the zucchini, tomatoes, green beans, peas, and black pepper; cook until the vegetables are tender, about 10 minutes longer. Remove from the heat; stir in the basil and sprinkle with the Swiss cheese.

Per serving (about 1 ¾ cups): 133 Cal, 1 g Fat, 1 g Sat Fat, 0 g Trans Fat, 3 mg Chol, 653 mg Sod, 23 g Carb, 5 g Fib, 9 g Prot, 117 mg Calc. *PointsPlus* value: **3.**

Easy Garden Vegetable Soup

SERVES 4

3 large tomatoes, coarsely chopped

1 cup drained canned diced tomatoes

½ English (seedless) cucumber, coarsely chopped

½ small red onion, coarsely chopped

¼ cup lightly packed torn fresh basil

2 tablespoons drained jarred chopped pimiento

¼ cup water

2 tablespoons red-wine vinegar

1 tablespoon olive oil

¼ teaspoon hot pepper sauce

½ teaspoon salt

Combine the fresh and canned tomatoes in a food processor and puree. Add the cucumber, onion, basil, and pimiento; pulse until pureed. Add the water, vinegar, oil, pepper sauce, and salt; process until blended. Serve at room temperature or refrigerate, covered, to serve cold.

Per serving (1 ¼ cups): 76 Cal, 4 g Fat, 1 g Sat Fat, 0 g Trans Fat, 0 mg Chol, 505 mg Sod, 10 g Carb, 2 g Fib, 2 g Prot, 22 mg Calc. *PointsPlus* value: **2.**

⏱ Time-Saver

To chill the soup in a hurry, pour it into a metal bowl and place the bowl in a larger bowl half-filled with ice water. Let stand, stirring occasionally, until cold, about 15 minutes.

Double Mushroom Broth with Soba Noodles

SERVES 4

8 ounces soba noodles

4 cups reduced-sodium chicken broth

4 quarter-size slices peeled fresh ginger, very thinly sliced

1 teaspoon reduced-sodium soy sauce

1 teaspoon Asian (dark) sesame oil

½ pound firm tofu, cut into ¾-inch chunks

1 cup drained canned straw mushrooms

1 cup enoki mushrooms, trimmed

¼ cup chopped chives

1 Bring a large pot of salted water to a boil. Add the noodles and cook according to the package directions; drain and set aside.

2 Meanwhile, combine the broth, ginger, soy sauce, and sesame oil in a medium saucepan; bring to a boil over medium-high heat. Reduce the heat and simmer, covered, about 5 minutes. Stir in the tofu, straw mushrooms, and enoki mushrooms. Cook, covered, about 5 minutes longer. Remove the saucepan from the heat and stir in the chives.

3 Put ¾ cup of the soba noodles in each of 4 bowls and divide the broth, tofu, and mushrooms evenly among the bowls.

Per serving (1¼ cups): 275 Cal, 4 g Fat, 1 g Sat Fat, 0 g Trans Fat, 0 mg Chol, 1129 mg Sod, 47 g Carb, 3 g Fib, 17 g Prot, 138 mg Calc. **PointsPlus** value: **7.**

Double Mushroom Broth with Soba Noodles

Pork Chops with Corn–Bell Pepper Relish

Delicious Steaks, Chops, and More

Steak with Olive-Mint Sauce

Flank Steak with Chimichurri Sauce

Easy Pepper Steak

Onion-Smothered Sirloin Steak

Peppered Steak with
Brandy-Mustard Sauce

Moroccan-Style Beef Kebabs

Quick Burgundy-Style Beef Stew

Beef and Green Beans
with Asian Flavors

Garlicky Beef and Snow Peas

Japanese-Style Beef
and Vegetable Salad

North African—Style Burgers

Microwave Chili-Stuffed Tomatoes

Tex-Mex Beef and Vegetable Salad

Pork Chops with
Corn—Bell Pepper Relish

Pork Chops with
Fresh Herb Vinaigrette

Skillet Pork Chops with
Apricot-Mustard Sauce

Pork with Cauliflower and Walnuts

Salad-Topped Pork Cutlets

Pork Tenderloin with Cranberry
Pan Sauce and Butternut Squash

Pork Medallions with
Fresh Pear Chutney

Sautéed Pork with Peaches

Stir-Fried Pork and Broccoli
with Hoisin Sauce

Black Pepper Pork with Scallions

Glazed Ham Steak with
Summer Fruit Relish

Pork with Ginger and Noodles

Broiled Lamb Chops
with Parsley-Walnut Pesto

Lamb with Cucumber-Radish Salad

Pressure Cooker
Moroccan-Style Lamb

Hunan-Style Lamb and Bell Peppers

Easy Moussaka

Lamb Burgers with Garlicky
Yogurt Sauce

Veal Cutlets with
Lemon-Caper Sauce

Steak with Olive-Mint Sauce

SERVES 4

1 (1-pound) flank steak, trimmed

⅛ teaspoon salt

¼ teaspoon black pepper

½ cup reduced-sodium beef broth

2 tablespoons finely chopped green olives

2 tablespoons finely chopped dry-packed sun-dried tomatoes

2 tablespoons chopped fresh mint

1 Spray the rack of a broiler pan with olive oil nonstick spray and preheat the broiler.

2 Sprinkle the steak with the salt and pepper. Place on the broiler rack and broil 4 inches from the heat until an instant-read thermometer inserted into the side of the steak registers 145°F for medium, about 5 minutes on each side.

3 Meanwhile, combine the broth, olives, and sun-dried tomatoes in a small saucepan; bring to a boil. Cook until the liquid is reduced by half and the tomatoes are softened, about 5 minutes; stir in the mint.

4 Slice the steak across the grain into 16 slices. Divide evenly among 4 plates and top with the sauce.

Per serving (4 slices steak and 2 tablespoons sauce): 197 Cal, 8 g Fat, 3 g Sat Fat, 0 g Trans Fat, 49 mg Chol, 209 mg Sod, 2 g Carb, 1 g Fib, 27 g Prot, 18 mg Calc. *PointsPlus* value: **4.**

◆ Filling Extra

Round out the meal with cooked small potatoes and steamed broccoli florets (5 ounces cooked small potatoes for each serving will increase the *PointsPlus* value by **3**).

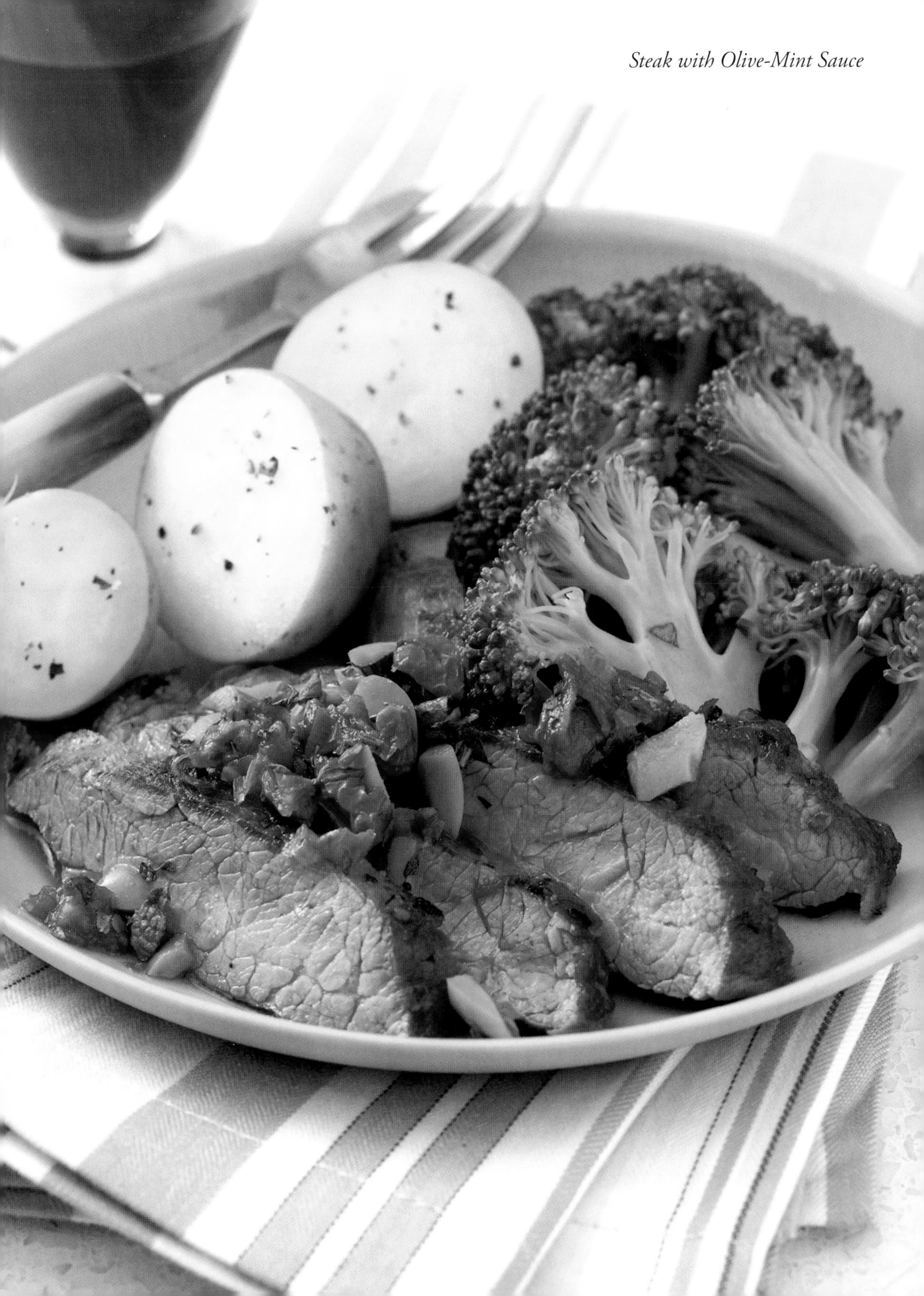

Steak with Olive-Mint Sauce

Flank Steak with Chimichurri Sauce

SERVES 6

¼ cup lightly packed chopped fresh cilantro

¼ cup lightly packed chopped fresh parsley

1 garlic clove, minced

2 tablespoons red-wine vinegar

1 tablespoon olive oil

1 teaspoon salt

¼ teaspoon crushed red pepper

1 tablespoon taco or Mexican seasoning

1 (1¼-pound) flank steak, trimmed

1 Spray the rack of a broiler pan with olive oil nonstick spray and preheat the broiler.

2 To make the chimichurri sauce, combine the cilantro, parsley, garlic, vinegar, oil, ½ teaspoon of the salt, and the crushed red pepper in a small bowl; set aside.

3 Combine the taco seasoning and the remaining ½ teaspoon salt in a cup. Rub on the steak.

4 Place the steak on the broiler rack and broil about 5 inches from the heat until an instant-read thermometer inserted into the side of the steak registers 145°F for medium, about 5 minutes on each side. Slice against the grain into 18 slices. Serve with the chimichurri sauce.

Per serving (3 slices steak and about 5 teaspoons chimichurri sauce): 169 Cal, 9 g Fat, 3 g Sat Fat, 1 g Trans Fat, 45 mg Chol, 541 mg Sod, 2 g Carb, 0 g Fib, 19 g Prot, 11 mg Calc. *PointsPlus* value: **4.**

🕐 Time-Saver

To get a jump-start on the prep, make the chimichurri sauce up to 2 hours ahead and store, covered, in the refrigerator.

Easy Pepper Steak

SERVES 6

- 1¾ cups reduced-sodium beef broth
- 2 tablespoons reduced-sodium soy sauce
- 1½ tablespoons cornstarch
- 2 teaspoons canola oil
- 1 pound flank steak, trimmed and thinly sliced against the grain
- 4 assorted-color bell peppers, cut into thin strips
- 6 scallions, cut into 2-inch lengths
- 2 garlic cloves, minced

1 Stir together 1¼ cups of the broth, the soy sauce, and cornstarch in a small bowl until smooth; set aside.

2 Heat the oil in a nonstick wok or large deep nonstick skillet over high heat. Add the steak and stir-fry until browned, about 4 minutes. Transfer to a medium bowl; set aside.

3 Add the bell peppers to the wok and stir-fry until crisp-tender, about 3 minutes. Add the scallions and garlic; stir-fry about 1 minute. Add the remaining ½ cup broth; cook, covered, about 3 minutes. Return the beef to the wok. Stir the cornstarch mixture and add to the wok; stir-fry until the sauce thickens and bubbles, about 1 minute longer.

Per serving (about 1¼ cups): 183 Cal, 5 g Fat, 1 g Sat Fat, 0 g Trans Fat, 55 mg Chol, 261 mg Sod, 9 g Carb, 2 g Fib, 25 g Prot, 26 mg Calc. *PointsPlus* value: **4.**

◆ *Filling Extra*

Serve with bulgur for sopping up all the flavorful sauce (½ cup cooked bulgur for each serving will increase the *PointsPlus* value by **2**).

Onion-Smothered Sirloin Steak

SERVES 4

3 teaspoons olive oil

2 large onions, thinly sliced

4 garlic cloves, minced

½ teaspoon dried thyme

¾ teaspoon salt

¼ teaspoon black pepper

1 cup reduced-sodium beef broth

2 (½-pound) boneless sirloin steaks, trimmed and cut crosswise in half

1 Heat 2 teaspoons of the oil in a large nonstick skillet over medium-high heat. Add the onions, garlic, thyme, ¼ teaspoon of the salt, and ⅛ teaspoon of the pepper; cook, stirring occasionally, until the onions are soft and golden, about 8 minutes. Add the broth and cook until almost evaporated, about 4 minutes. Transfer to a medium bowl; set aside.

2 Meanwhile, heat the remaining 1 teaspoon oil in another large nonstick skillet over medium-high heat. Sprinkle the steaks with the remaining ½ teaspoon salt and ⅛ teaspoon pepper. Add to the skillet and cook until browned, about 2 minutes on each side. Add the onion mixture and cook, stirring to scrape up any browned bits from the bottom of the pan, until the steaks are cooked to medium doneness, about 2 minutes longer.

Per serving (½ steak and about ¼ cup onion mixture): 221 Cal, 8 g Fat, 2 g Sat Fat, 0 g Trans Fat, 66 mg Chol, 523 mg Sod, 9 g Carb, 2 g Fib, 29 g Prot, 31 mg Calc. **PointsPlus** value: **5.**

⏱ Time-Saver

Slice the onions in a food processor and transfer to a bowl. Replace the slicing blade with the chopping blade, then add the garlic, one clove at a time, and process until minced.

Peppered Steak with Brandy-Mustard Sauce

SERVES 4

1 tablespoon whole black peppercorns, crushed

4 (¼-pound) filets mignons, trimmed

2 large zucchini, halved lengthwise and thinly sliced

4 shallots, minced

3 tablespoons brandy

½ cup reduced-sodium beef broth

1 tablespoon coarse-grained Dijon mustard

½ teaspoon salt

1 Put the peppercorns on a plate; lightly press both sides of the steak into the peppercorns to coat evenly.

2 Spray a large nonstick skillet with nonstick spray and set over medium-high heat. Add the steaks and cook until an instant-read thermometer inserted in the side of a steak registers 145°F for medium, about 5 minutes on each side. Transfer to a platter and keep warm.

3 Add the zucchini and shallots to the skillet; cook, stirring, until softened, about 3 minutes. Add the brandy and cook about 20 seconds. (If the brandy ignites, cover the skillet with the lid and remove it from the heat until the flame is extinguished.) Stir in the broth, mustard, and salt. Simmer until the sauce is slightly thickened, about 3 minutes. Spoon the vegetables and sauce over the steaks.

Per serving (1 steak and about 1 cup vegetables with sauce): 239 Cal, 8 g Fat, 3 g Sat Fat, 0 g Trans Fat, 46 mg Chol, 463 mg Sod, 11 g Carb, 3 g Fib, 28 g Prot, 50 mg Calc. **PointsPlus** value: **7.**

⏱ Time-Saver

Substitute 2 teaspoons cracked black pepper (from a jar) for the whole black peppercorns to save having to crush them.

Quick Burgundy-Style Beef Stew

SERVES 4

1 pound beef tenderloin, trimmed and cut into 1-inch chunks

½ teaspoon salt

¼ teaspoon black pepper

1 (12-ounce) package frozen mixed vegetables, preferably with pearl onions and carrots, thawed

1 (10-ounce) package white mushrooms, halved or quartered if large

1 teaspoon dried thyme

⅔ cup dry red wine

1 cup canned reduced-sodium fat-free beef gravy

1 Sprinkle the beef with the salt and pepper; set aside.

2 Spray a nonstick Dutch oven with nonstick spray and set over medium-high heat. Add the beef and cook until browned on all sides, about 2 minutes. Add the mixed vegetables, mushrooms, and thyme; cook, stirring, about 1 minute.

3 Add the wine to the Dutch oven and bring to a boil, scraping up any browned bits from the bottom of the pot. Reduce the heat and simmer about 2 minutes. Stir in the gravy and bring to a boil. Reduce the heat and simmer until the mushrooms are tender and the sauce is slightly thickened, about 5 minutes longer.

Per serving (1½ cups): 233 Cal, 8 g Fat, 3 g Sat Fat, 0 g Trans Fat, 46 mg Chol, 369 mg Sod, 11 g Carb, 3 g Fib, 29 g Prot, 40 mg Calc. *PointsPlus* value: **7.**

◆ Filling Extra

Coarsely mash 2 cooked medium potatoes, season with salt and pepper, and serve with the stew. This will increase the per-serving *PointsPlus* value by **2.**

Beef and Green Beans with Asian Flavors

SERVES 4

2 tablespoons shredded
 unsweetened coconut

1 pound round steak, trimmed
 and cut into thin strips

1 teaspoon cinnamon

¼ teaspoon five-spice powder

¾ pound thin green beans

1 cup cherry tomatoes

¼ cup reduced-sodium beef
 broth

2 tablespoons Asian fish sauce

1 teaspoon Asian red chili sauce

2 cups hot cooked
 quick-cooking brown rice

1 Put the coconut in a spice grinder or mini–food processor and finely grind.

2 Toss together the beef, coconut, cinnamon, and five-spice powder in a medium bowl until coated.

3 Spray a large nonstick skillet with nonstick spray and set over medium-high heat. Add the beef and cook, stirring, until browned, about 4 minutes. Transfer to a plate; set aside.

4 Add the green beans and tomatoes to the skillet and cook, stirring, about 2 minutes. Add the broth, fish sauce, and chili sauce. Bring to a simmer and cook, stirring to scrape up any browned bits from the bottom of the pan, until the beans are tender, about 4 minutes.

5 Return the beef and any accumulated juices to the skillet. Cook until the beef is heated through and the sauce is slightly thickened, about 2 minutes longer. Serve with the rice.

Per serving (1½ cups): 340 Cal, 7 g Fat, 3 g Sat Fat, 0 g Trans Fat, 81 mg Chol, 779 mg Sod, 31 g Carb, 7 g Fib, 38 g Prot, 63 mg Calc. **PointsPlus** value: **8.**

⏱ Time-Saver

Look for prepackaged thin-sliced top-round steak at the supermarket and cut it into strips.

Garlicky Beef and Snow Peas

SERVES 4

5 garlic cloves, minced

1 tablespoon minced peeled fresh ginger

¾ pound boneless sirloin steak, trimmed and cut into thin strips

4 scallions, cut into 1½-inch lengths

1½ cups snow peas, trimmed

1 large red bell pepper, thinly sliced

⅓ cup reduced-sodium chicken broth

2 tablespoons reduced-sodium soy sauce

1 teaspoon sugar

1½ teaspoons cornstarch

1 tablespoon water

½–1 teaspoon chili garlic sauce

1 Spray a nonstick wok or large deep nonstick skillet with nonstick spray and set over high heat. When a drop of water sizzles in it, add the garlic and ginger; stir-fry until fragrant, about 1 minute. Add the beef and stir-fry until browned, about 3 minutes. Add the scallions, snow peas, and bell pepper; stir-fry about 1 minute. Add the broth, soy sauce, and sugar; bring to a simmer. Reduce the heat and simmer, stirring occasionally, about 2 minutes.

2 Meanwhile, stir together the cornstarch, water, and chili sauce in a cup until smooth. Add to the wok and stir-fry until the sauce thickens and bubbles, about 30 seconds.

Per serving (1 cup): 159 Cal, 3 g Fat, 1 g Sat Fat, 0 g Trans Fat, 50 mg Chol, 352 mg Sod, 10 g Carb, 2 g Fib, 22 g Prot, 37 mg Calc. **PointsPlus** value: **4.**

◆ *Filling Extra*

Spoon this boldly flavored stir-fry over brown rice (½ cup cooked brown rice for each serving will increase the **PointsPlus** value by **3**).

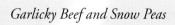

Japanese-Style Beef and Vegetable Salad

SERVES 4

1 tablespoon powdered green tea

2 teaspoons wasabi powder

1 teaspoon sugar

4 (3-ounce) filets mignons, trimmed

6 cups coleslaw mix

2 cups packaged matchstick-cut carrots

8 white mushrooms, sliced

1 tablespoon reduced-sodium soy sauce

1 tablespoon unseasoned rice vinegar

2 teaspoons canola oil

1 teaspoon Asian (dark) sesame oil

1 Combine the powdered green tea, wasabi powder, and sugar on a plate. Press both sides of the steaks into the mixture to coat evenly.

2 Spray a large nonstick skillet with nonstick spray and set over medium-high heat. Add the steaks and cook until an instant-read thermometer inserted into the side of a steak registers 145°F for medium, about 4 minutes on each side.

3 Meanwhile, combine the coleslaw mix, carrots, and mushrooms in a large bowl. Add the soy sauce, vinegar, canola oil, and sesame oil; toss to coat.

4 Thinly slice the steaks. Divide the salad evenly among 4 plates and top each with a sliced steak.

Per serving (about 2 cups salad and 1 sliced steak): 237 Cal, 9 g Fat, 2 g Sat Fat, 0 g Trans Fat, 35 mg Chol, 289 mg Sod, 17 g Carb, 5 g Fib, 22 g Prot, 72 mg Calc. **PointsPlus** value: **6.**

North African–Style Burgers

SERVES 4

1 pound ground lean beef (7% fat or less)

1 tablespoon tomato paste

1 teaspoon ground cumin

½ teaspoon cinnamon

¾ teaspoon salt

¼ teaspoon black pepper

4 whole-wheat hamburger buns, split

4 tomato slices

4 sweet onion slices

4 green leaf lettuce leaves

1 Combine the beef, tomato paste, cumin, cinnamon, salt, and pepper in a medium bowl. With damp hands, shape the mixture into 4 (½-inch-thick) patties.

2 Spray a large nonstick skillet with nonstick spray and set over medium heat. Add the patties and cook until an instant-read thermometer inserted into the side of a burger registers 160°F, about 4 minutes on each side.

3 Put a burger on the bottom half of each bun and top with 1 tomato slice, 1 onion slice, and 1 lettuce leaf. Cover with the tops of the buns.

Per serving (1 garnished burger): 280 Cal, 8 g Fat, 3 g Sat Fat, 1 g Trans Fat, 64 mg Chol, 735 mg Sod, 22 g Carb, 4 g Fib, 29 g Prot, 79 mg Calc. **PointsPlus** value: **7.**

⏱ Time-Saver

Use an ice-cream scoop to quickly and accurately divide the beef mixture before shaping it into the patties.

Microwave Chili-Stuffed Tomatoes

SERVES 4

4 large tomatoes

1 small onion, chopped

2 garlic cloves, minced

½ pound ground lean beef
(7% fat or less)

1 cup canned red kidney beans,
rinsed and drained

1½ tablespoons chili powder

½ teaspoon dried oregano

½ teaspoon salt

4 tablespoons shredded
fat-free Monterey Jack cheese

1 Cut off and discard a slice from the top of each tomato. With a small spoon, remove the seeds and inner flesh; discard the seeds and chop the flesh.

2 Spray a large nonstick skillet with olive oil nonstick spray and set over medium-high heat. Add the onion and cook, stirring, until softened, about 4 minutes. Add the garlic and cook, stirring, until fragrant, about 20 seconds. Add the beef and cook, breaking it apart with a wooden spoon, until browned, about 3 minutes.

3 Stir in the beans, chopped tomato, chili powder, oregano, and salt; cook, stirring, until heated through, about 2 minutes. Remove the skillet from the heat and stir in a tablespoon or two of water if the mixture seems dry.

4 Spoon the beef mixture evenly into the tomatoes; sprinkle evenly with the Jack cheese. Place the stuffed tomatoes in a microwavable dish; microwave on High until the tomatoes soften but still hold their shape and the cheese melts, about 5 minutes. Let stand about 1 minute at room temperature before serving.

Per serving (1 stuffed tomato): 204 Cal, 4 g Fat, 2 g Sat Fat, 0 g Trans Fat, 34 mg Chol, 634 mg Sod, 24 g Carb, 6 g Fib, 18 g Prot, 112 mg Calc. *PointsPlus* value: **6.**

Tex-Mex Beef and Vegetable Salad

SERVES 4

¾ pound ground lean beef (7% fat or less)

2 teaspoons chili powder

½ teaspoon salt

½ head romaine lettuce, thinly sliced

2 large tomatoes, cut into ¼-inch dice

1 (15-ounce) can black beans, rinsed and drained

1 large Granny Smith apple, cored and cut into matchsticks

1 red onion, cut into ¼-inch dice

1¼ cups prepared fat-free salsa

½ cup fat-free sour cream

¼ cup lightly packed fresh cilantro leaves (optional)

1 Spray a large nonstick skillet with olive oil nonstick spray and set over medium heat. Add the beef and cook, breaking it apart with a wooden spoon, until browned, about 3 minutes. Stir in the chili powder and salt; cook, stirring, until fragrant, about 1 minute. Remove the skillet from the heat; let stand about 5 minutes.

2 Layer the lettuce, tomatoes, beans, apple, and onion in a large glass bowl or large round casserole dish. Top with the beef mixture.

3 Spoon the salsa and sour cream on top of the salad; sprinkle with the cilantro, if using.

Per serving (about 1 ¾ cups): 334 Cal, 6 g Fat, 2 g Sat Fat, 0 g Trans Fat, 51 mg Chol, 1162 mg Sod, 45 g Carb, 14 g Fib, 27 g Prot, 163 mg Calc. **PointsPlus** value: **8.**

Pork Chops with Corn—Bell Pepper Relish

SERVES 4

2 cups fresh or frozen corn
   kernels

1 small red bell pepper, chopped

2 small scallions, chopped

2 tablespoons honey

2 tablespoons white vinegar

¾ teaspoon salt

¼ teaspoon black pepper

Pinch cayenne

4 (¼-pound) thin-cut boneless
   pork loin chops, trimmed

2 teaspoons olive oil

1 Combine the corn, bell pepper, scallions, honey, vinegar, ½ teaspoon of the salt, ⅛ teaspoon of the black pepper, and the cayenne in a medium saucepan and set over medium heat. Cook, stirring occasionally, until tender, about 5 minutes; remove the saucepan from the heat; set aside.

2 Sprinkle the pork chops with the remaining ¼ teaspoon salt and ⅛ teaspoon black pepper. Heat the oil in a large nonstick skillet over medium-high heat. Add the pork chops and cook until browned and cooked through, about 3 minutes on each side. Serve with the relish.

Per serving (1 chop and about ¾ cup relish): 307 Cal, 10 g Fat, 3 g Sat Fat, 0 g Trans Fat, 70 mg Chol, 687 mg Sod, 29 g Carb, 3 g Fib, 29 g Prot, 34 mg Calc. **PointsPlus** value: **7.**

⏱ Time-Saver

Prepare the relish and refrigerate in an airtight container up to 1 day ahead.

Pork Chops with
Corn–Bell Pepper Relish

Pork Chops with Fresh Herb Vinaigrette

SERVES 4

3 tablespoons reduced-sodium chicken broth

1 tablespoon olive oil

1 shallot, finely chopped

1 garlic clove, minced

2 teaspoons grated lemon zest

1 tablespoon lemon juice

¼ cup chopped mixed fresh herbs, such as mint, parsley, chives, and tarragon

¾ teaspoon salt

Pinch cayenne

4 (¼-pound) boneless pork loin chops, trimmed

½ teaspoon black pepper

1 To make the vinaigrette, whisk together the broth, oil, shallot, garlic, lemon zest and juice, herbs, ¼ teaspoon of the salt, and the cayenne in a small bowl; set aside.

2 Sprinkle the pork chops with the remaining ½ teaspoon salt and the pepper. Spray a large nonstick skillet with olive oil nonstick spray and set over medium-high heat. Add the pork chops and cook until an instant-read thermometer inserted into the side of a chop registers 160°F for medium, about 4 minutes on each side. Transfer to a platter. Re-whisk the vinaigrette and spoon over the chops.

Per serving (1 pork chop and about 1 tablespoon vinaigrette): 171 Cal, 10 g Fat, 3 g Sat Fat, 0 g Trans Fat, 51 mg Chol, 502 mg Sod, 2 g Carb, 0 g Fib, 18 g Prot, 16 mg Calc. *PointsPlus* value: **5.**

◆ Filling Extra

A side of steamed sliced zucchini and red bell pepper is the perfect accompaniment for this pork.

Skillet Pork Chops with Apricot-Mustard Sauce

SERVES 4

½ cup apricot jam

2 tablespoons coarse-grained Dijon mustard

1 tablespoon reduced-sodium soy sauce

2 tablespoons lime juice

1 garlic clove, minced

Pinch cayenne

4 (5-ounce) thin-cut bone-in pork loin chops

½ teaspoon salt

¼ teaspoon black pepper

1 teaspoon canola oil

1 Combine the jam, mustard, soy sauce, lime juice, garlic, and cayenne in a small bowl; set aside.

2 Sprinkle the pork chops with the salt and pepper. Heat the oil in a large nonstick skillet over medium-high heat. Add the pork chops and cook until browned and cooked through, 4–5 minutes on each side; transfer to a platter and keep warm. Add the jam mixture to the skillet and bring to a boil. Reduce the heat and simmer until the sauce thickens slightly, about 3 minutes. Spoon the sauce over the chops.

Per serving (1 pork chop and about 3 tablespoons sauce): 264 Cal, 6 g Fat, 2 g Sat Fat, 0 g Trans Fat, 56 mg Chol, 541 mg Sod, 30 g Carb, 1 g Fib, 21 g Prot, 40 mg Calc. *PointsPlus* value: **8.**

Time-Saver

Substitute apple-cider vinegar for the lime juice.

Pork with Cauliflower and Walnuts

SERVES 4

4 (¼-pound) boneless pork loin chops, trimmed

1 teaspoon salt

¼ teaspoon black pepper

3 cups cauliflower florets

¼ cup reduced-sodium chicken broth

2 large oranges, peeled and sectioned

2 tablespoons chopped walnuts

1 Place the pork chops between sheets of wax paper. With a meat mallet or rolling pin, pound the chops to ¼-inch thickness. Season with the salt and pepper.

2 Spray a large nonstick skillet with nonstick spray and set over medium heat. Add the pork chops and cook until browned and cooked through, about 2 minutes on each side. Transfer to a platter; set aside.

3 Add the cauliflower and broth to the skillet; cook, covered, until the cauliflower is tender, about 5 minutes. Add the orange sections, walnuts, pork, and any accumulated juices. Cook until heated through, about 1 minute longer.

Per serving (1 pork chop and ½ cup vegetables with sauce): 267 Cal, 11 g Fat, 3 g Sat Fat, 0 g Trans Fat, 70 mg Chol, 689 mg Sod, 15 g Carb, 4 g Fib, 27 g Prot, 64 mg Calc. *PointsPlus* value: **6.**

Time-Saver

Look for packaged cauliflower florets right next to the bagged salads in the supermarket's produce section.

Salad-Topped Pork Cutlets

SERVES 4

¾ cup Italian-seasoned dried bread crumbs

4 (¼-pound) slices boneless pork loin

¾ teaspoon salt

½ teaspoon black pepper

2 tablespoons reduced-fat mayonnaise

2 tablespoons red-wine vinegar

2 teaspoons olive oil

2 teaspoons water

1 teaspoon Dijon mustard

6 cups mixed baby salad greens

1 small red onion, thinly sliced

12 cherry tomatoes, halved

1 Spray the rack of a broiler pan with nonstick spray and preheat the broiler.

2 Put the bread crumbs on a sheet of wax paper. Sprinkle the pork with ½ teaspoon of the salt and ¼ teaspoon of the pepper. Brush both sides with the mayonnaise, then coat evenly with the bread crumbs, pressing lightly so they adhere.

3 Place the cutlets on the broiler rack and broil 4 inches from the heat until browned and cooked through, about 3 minutes on each side.

4 Meanwhile, whisk together the vinegar, oil, water, mustard, and the remaining ¼ teaspoon salt and ¼ teaspoon pepper in a large bowl. Add the salad greens, onion, and tomatoes; toss to coat evenly. Place a cutlet on each of 4 plates and top evenly with the salad.

Per serving (1 pork cutlet and generous 1½ cups salad): 338 Cal, 15 g Fat, 4 g Sat Fat, 0 g Trans Fat, 72 mg Chol, 834 mg Sod, 22 g Carb, 4 g Fib, 29 g Prot, 99 mg Calc. *PointsPlus* value: **8.**

Pork Tenderloin with Cranberry Pan Sauce and Butternut Squash

SERVES 4

1¼ pounds pork tenderloin, trimmed and cut into 8 slices

1 teaspoon salt

¼ teaspoon black pepper

½ cup reduced-sodium vegetable broth

¼ cup whole-berry cranberry sauce

1 tablespoon grated orange zest

½ teaspoon dried thyme

1 (10-ounce) package frozen butternut squash puree, thawed

¾ teaspoon pumpkin pie spice

2 teaspoons unsalted butter

1 Spray a large nonstick skillet with nonstick spray and set over medium-high heat. Sprinkle the pork with ½ teaspoon of the salt and the pepper. Add to the skillet and cook until browned, about 2 minutes on each side. Transfer to a plate.

2 Add the broth to the skillet, scraping up any browned bits from the bottom of the pan. Add the cranberry sauce, orange zest, thyme, and pork along with any accumulated juices; bring to a boil. Reduce the heat and simmer, covered, until the pork is cooked through, about 8 minutes.

3 Meanwhile, combine the squash puree, pumpkin pie spice, and the remaining ½ teaspoon salt in a microwavable bowl. Dot with the butter. Microwave on High 30 seconds. Stir, then microwave, stirring twice more, until heated through, 2–3 minutes.

4 Divide the squash puree evenly among 4 plates and top evenly with the pork and sauce.

Per serving (2 pieces pork, 2 tablespoons sauce, and ¼ cup squash puree): 264 Cal, 8 g Fat, 3 g Sat Fat, 0 g Trans Fat, 95 mg Chol, 728 mg Sod, 14 g Carb, 3 g Fib, 33 g Prot, 28 mg Calc. **PointsPlus** value: **6.**

◆ Filling Extra

Serve with 2 cups of steamed green beans seasoned with salt and pepper to taste and a squeeze of fresh lemon juice.

*Pork Tenderloin with Cranberry Pan Sauce
and Butternut Squash*

Pork Medallions with Fresh Pear Chutney

SERVES 4

¾ pound pork tenderloin, trimmed and cut into 1-inch slices

½ teaspoon salt

¼ teaspoon black pepper

2 teaspoons olive oil

2 firm-ripe pears, peeled, halved, cored, and chopped

2 teaspoons grated peeled fresh ginger

¼ cup mango chutney

¼ cup reduced-sodium chicken broth

1 Sprinkle the pork with the salt and pepper. Heat 1 teaspoon of the oil in a large nonstick skillet over medium-high heat. Add the pork and cook until browned and cooked through, about 3 minutes on each side. Transfer to a platter and keep warm.

2 Add the remaining 1 teaspoon oil to the skillet. Add the pears and ginger; cook, stirring, until the pears are tender and golden, about 5 minutes. Stir in the chutney and broth; bring to a boil, scraping up the browned bits from the bottom of the pan. Cook until the sauce thickens slightly, about 5 minutes. Spoon the chutney over the pork.

Per serving (about 2 slices pork and ½ cup chutney): 201 Cal, 6 g Fat, 1 g Sat Fat, 0 g Trans Fat, 54 mg Chol, 411 mg Sod, 18 g Carb, 2 g Fib, 19 g Prot, 29 mg Calc. **PointsPlus** value: **5.**

Sautéed Pork with Peaches

SERVES 4

1½ pounds pork tenderloin, trimmed and cut into 8 slices

¾ teaspoon salt

¼ teaspoon black pepper

1 teaspoon canola oil

1 red onion, thinly sliced

2 peaches, cut into ½-inch wedges

½ cup dry red wine

2 tablespoons lemon juice

2 tablespoons packed brown sugar

⅛ teaspoon cinnamon

1 Place the slices of pork between sheets of wax paper. With a meat mallet or rolling pin, pound to ¼-inch thickness.

2 Sprinkle the pork with the salt and pepper. Heat the oil in a large nonstick skillet over medium-high heat. Add the pork and cook until browned, about 2 minutes on each side; transfer to a plate.

3 Add the onion to the skillet; reduce the heat to medium and cook, stirring, until slightly softened, about 2 minutes. Add the peaches and cook, stirring, until lightly browned, about 2 minutes. Add the remaining ingredients and cook, stirring, about 1 minute. Return the pork to the skillet and simmer until cooked through, about 3 minutes.

Per serving (2 slices pork and about ⅓ cup peaches and sauce): 300 Cal, 9 g Fat, 3 g Sat Fat, 0 g Trans Fat, 107 mg Chol, 525 mg Sod, 16 g Carb, 1 g Fib, 37 g Prot, 34 mg Calc. **PointsPlus** value: **8.**

Stir-Fried Pork and Broccoli with Hoisin Sauce

SERVES 4

¾ pound boneless pork loin, trimmed and cut into 2 x ¼-inch strips

2 tablespoons dry sherry

1 tablespoon reduced-sodium soy sauce

1 tablespoon cornstarch

¾ teaspoon salt

¼ teaspoon black pepper

1 teaspoon Asian (dark) sesame oil

2 cups broccoli florets

1 orange bell pepper, cut into strips

1½ teaspoons grated peeled fresh ginger

¼ cup orange juice

¼ cup hoisin sauce

2 tablespoons honey

2 cups hot cooked white rice

1 Toss together the pork, sherry, soy sauce, cornstarch, salt, and black pepper in a large bowl until coated evenly; set aside.

2 Heat the sesame oil in a nonstick wok or large deep nonstick skillet over high heat. When a drop of water sizzles in it, add the broccoli and bell pepper; stir-fry about 2 minutes. Add the pork and stir-fry until browned, about 3 minutes. Add the ginger and stir-fry about 1 minute. Add the orange juice, hoisin sauce, and honey; stir-fry until the pork is cooked through and the sauce thickens and bubbles, about 2 minutes longer. Serve with the hot cooked rice.

Per serving (about 1 cup pork mixture and ½ cup rice): 313 Cal, 6 g Fat, 2 g Sat Fat, 0 g Trans Fat, 54 mg Chol, 453 mg Sod, 43 g Carb, 3 g Fib, 22 g Prot, 51 mg Calc. **PointsPlus** value: **8.**

Black Pepper Pork with Scallions

SERVES 4

- 8 scallions, sliced
- 1 large red bell pepper, cut into ½-inch pieces
- 4 garlic cloves, minced
- 1¼ pounds pork tenderloin, trimmed and cut into 2 x ¼-inch strips
- 4 teaspoons sugar
- ¼ cup reduced-sodium chicken broth
- 2 tablespoons Asian fish sauce
- 1¼ teaspoons black pepper or to taste

1 Spray a nonstick wok or large deep nonstick skillet with nonstick spray and set over high heat. Add the scallions, bell pepper, and garlic; stir-fry until tender, about 1 minute. Add the pork and stir-fry, until browned, about 3 minutes. Transfer to a large bowl; set aside.

2 Add the sugar to the wok and cook, stirring, until melted and light brown, about 30 seconds. Slowly stir in the broth (the caramel may form a hard lump). Cook, stirring constantly, until the sugar melts and the mixture begins to boil, about 20 seconds.

3 Stir in the fish sauce and black pepper; return the pork, vegetables, and any accumulated juices to the wok. Stir-fry until the sauce reduces to a glaze, about 2 minutes longer.

Per serving (1 cup): 222 Cal, 5 g Fat, 2 g Sat Fat, 0 g Trans Fat, 84 mg Chol, 796 mg Sod, 11 g Carb, 2 g Fib, 32 g Prot, 44 mg Calc. *PointsPlus* value: **5.**

Glazed Ham Steak with Summer Fruit Relish

SERVES 6

3 peaches, halved, pitted, and diced (about 2 cups)

1 (6-ounce) container blackberries, halved

1 cup small strawberries, hulled and quartered

¼ cup finely chopped red onion

2 tablespoons lemon juice

2 tablespoons chopped fresh mint

1 tablespoon Dijon mustard

1 tablespoon sugar

1 (1-pound) ham steak

1 Lightly spray the rack of a broiler pan with nonstick spray and preheat the broiler.

2 Combine the peaches, blackberries, strawberries, onion, lemon juice, and mint in a serving bowl; set aside.

3 Combine the mustard and sugar in a cup. Place the ham steak on the broiler rack and broil 4 inches from the heat 4 minutes. Turn and brush with the mustard mixture; broil until bubbly, about 4 minutes longer. Cut the steak into 6 equal portions and serve with the relish.

Per serving (⅙ of ham and about ⅔ cup fruit relish): 145 Cal, 3 g Fat, 1 g Sat Fat, 0 g Trans Fat, 40 mg Chol, 1,010 mg Sod, 16 g Carb, 2 g Fib, 14 g Prot, 12 mg Calc. **PointsPlus** value: **4.**

◆ Filling Extra

Enjoy the ham and relish along with a bowl of green peas steamed with thinly sliced butter lettuce, a classic French combination (½ cup cooked green peas for each serving will increase the **PointsPlus** value by **1**).

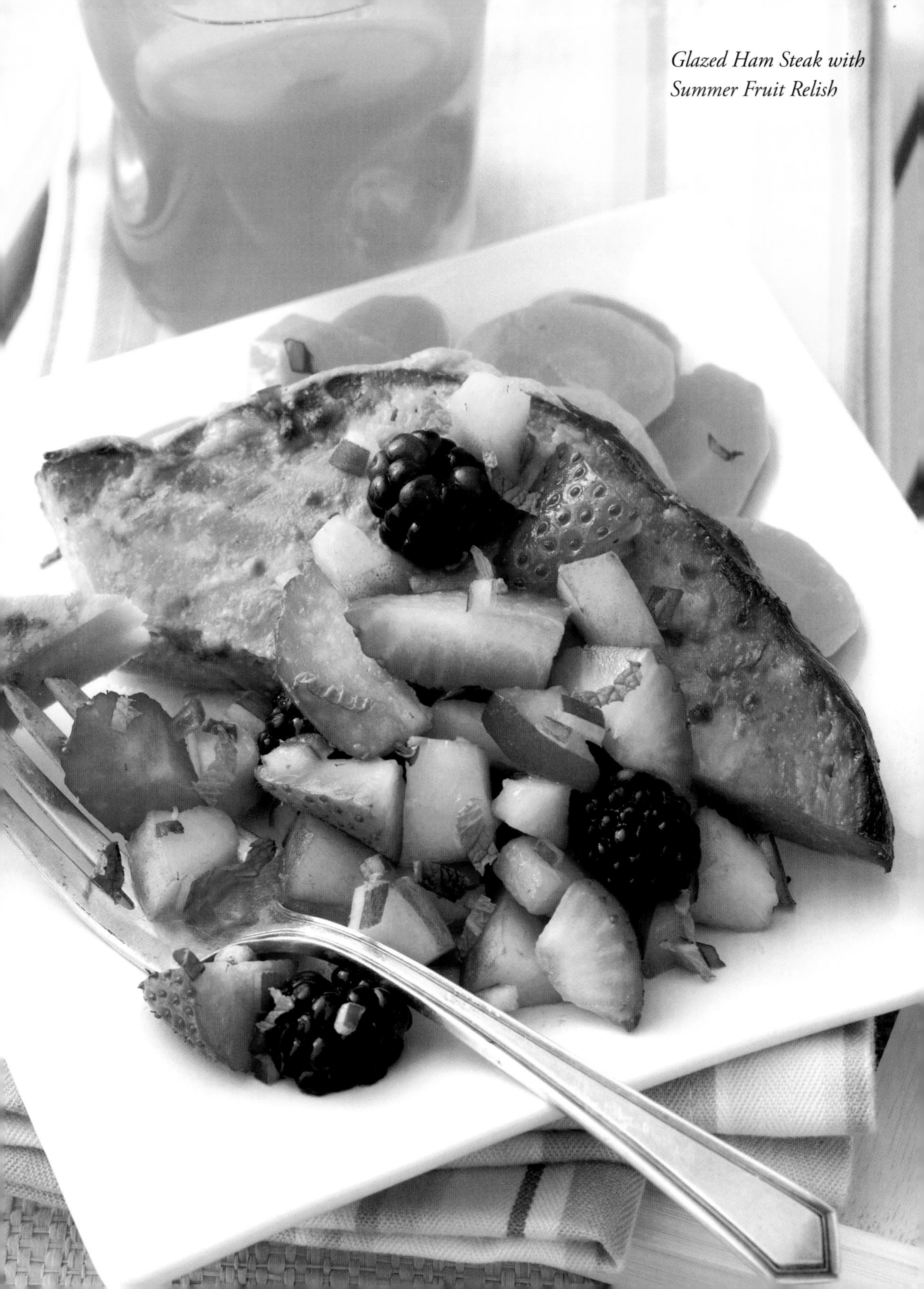

Glazed Ham Steak with Summer Fruit Relish

Pork with Ginger and Noodles

SERVES 4

¼ pound cellophane noodles

6 ounces ground lean pork

1 red onion, thinly sliced

2 tablespoons minced peeled fresh ginger

2 garlic cloves, minced

2 tablespoons reduced-sodium soy sauce

2 tablespoons red-wine vinegar

1 teaspoon Asian (dark) sesame oil

½ teaspoon crushed red pepper

⅓ cup reduced-sodium chicken broth

2 tablespoons chopped fresh cilantro

1 Put the noodles in a large bowl and add enough hot water to cover. Let soak until softened, about 10 minutes. Drain.

2 Meanwhile, spray a nonstick wok or large deep nonstick skillet with nonstick spray and set over medium-high heat. When a drop of water sizzles in it, add the pork and stir-fry, breaking it up with a wooden spoon, until browned, about 3 minutes.

3 Add the onion, ginger, and garlic to the wok; stir-fry until fragrant, about 30 seconds. Stir in the soy sauce, vinegar, sesame oil, and crushed red pepper. Pour in the broth, scraping up any browned bits from the bottom of the wok; bring the mixture to a simmer.

4 Add the noodles to the wok. Reduce the heat and simmer until all the liquid is absorbed, about 3 minutes. Sprinkle with the cilantro.

Per serving (¾ cup): 185 Cal, 5 g Fat, 1 g Sat Fat, 0 g Trans Fat, 27 mg Chol, 366 mg Sod, 24 g Carb, 2 g Fib, 12 g Prot, 29 mg Calc. **PointsPlus** value: **5.**

Broiled Lamb Chops with Parsley-Walnut Pesto

SERVES 4

4 (6-ounce) bone-in rib or lamb loin chops, trimmed

¾ teaspoon salt

¼ teaspoon black pepper

¾ cup finely chopped fresh parsley

3 tablespoons water

1½ tablespoons finely chopped walnuts

1 garlic clove, crushed through a press

2 teaspoons grated lemon zest

1 Spray the rack of a broiler pan with nonstick spray and preheat the broiler.

2 Sprinkle the lamb with ½ teaspoon of the salt and the pepper. Place on the broiler rack and broil 5 inches from the heat until an instant-read thermometer inserted into the side of a chop registers 145°F for medium, about 5 minutes on each side.

3 Meanwhile, to make the pesto, combine the parsley, water, walnuts, garlic, lemon zest, and the remaining ¼ teaspoon salt in a small bowl. Transfer the lamb chops to a platter and spoon the pesto evenly on top.

Per serving (1 lamb chop and 1½ tablespoons pesto): 159 Cal, 10 g Fat, 3 g Sat Fat, 1 g Trans Fat, 50 mg Chol, 492 mg Sod, 2 g Carb, 1 g Fib, 16 g Prot, 35 mg Calc. *PointsPlus* value: **4.**

◆ *Filling Extra*

A bowl of red or white quinoa makes an excellent side for these succulent chops (½ cup cooked quinoa per serving will increase the *PointsPlus* value by **3**).

Lamb with Cucumber-Radish Salad

SERVES 4

2 cucumbers, peeled, halved lengthwise, and thinly sliced

1 small red onion, thinly sliced

8 large radishes, thinly sliced, leaves coarsely chopped

1 tablespoon red-wine vinegar

¾ teaspoon salt

¼ teaspoon black pepper

1 teaspoon paprika

½ teaspoon chili powder

4 (5-ounce) lamb loin chops, trimmed

1 Spray the rack of a broiler pan with olive oil nonstick spray and preheat the broiler.

2 Combine the cucumbers, onion, radishes and their leaves, vinegar, ½ teaspoon of the salt, and ⅛ teaspoon of the pepper in a serving bowl; set aside.

3 Combine the paprika, chili powder, and the remaining ¼ teaspoon salt and ⅛ teaspoon pepper in a small bowl. Rub the spice mixture on the chops.

4 Place the lamb on the broiler rack and broil until an instant-read thermometer inserted into the side of a chop registers 145°F for medium, about 4 minutes on each side. Serve with the cucumber-radish salad.

Per serving (1 chop and 1 cup salad): 231 Cal, 10 g Fat, 3 g Sat Fat, 0 g Trans Fat, 93 mg Chol, 527 mg Sod, 5 g Carb, 2 g Fib, 30 g Prot, 34 mg Calc. **PointsPlus** value: **5.**

⏱ Time-Saver

Use a 10-inch length of English (seedless) cucumber instead of the regular cucumbers—there's no need to peel it.

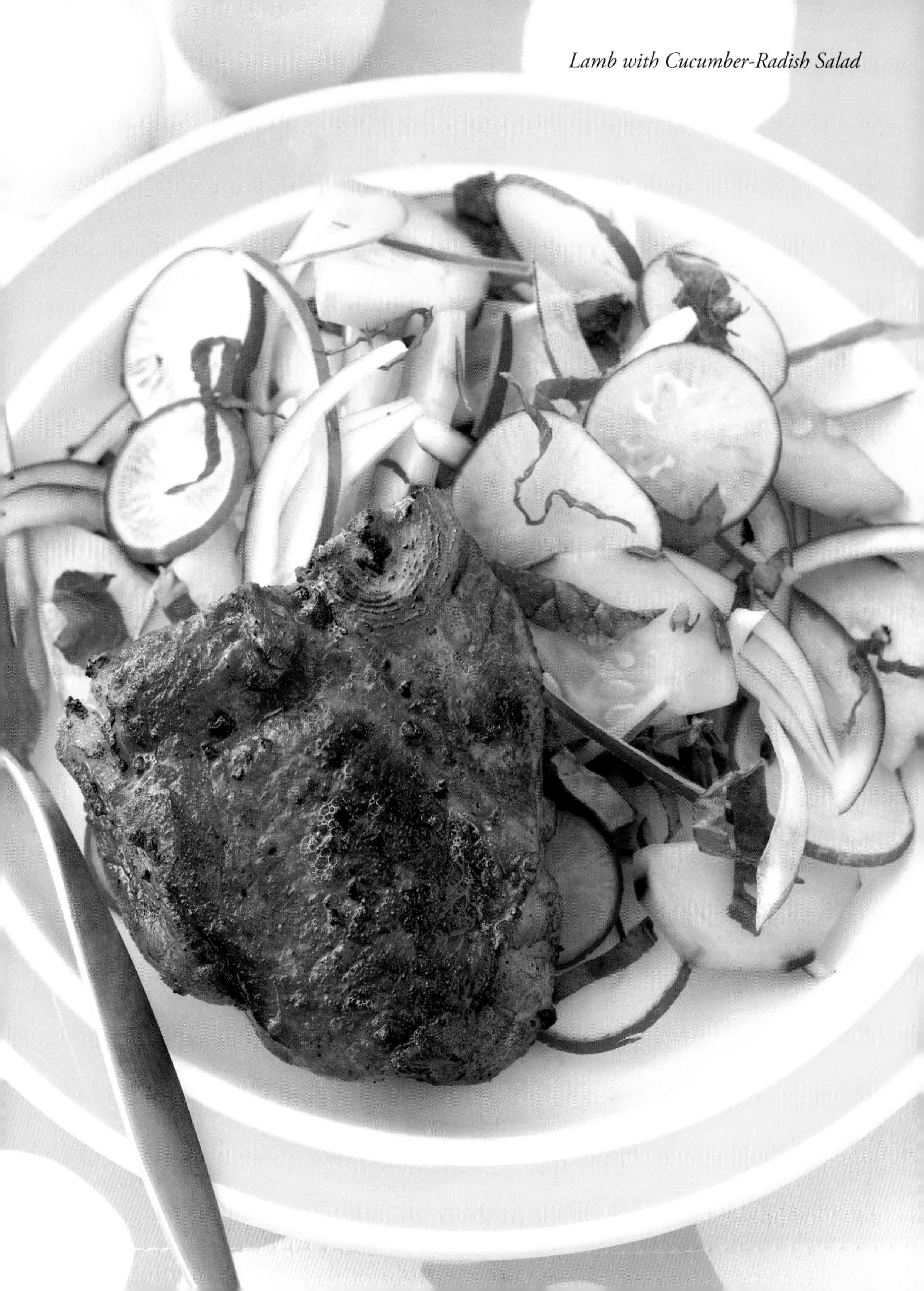

Lamb with Cucumber-Radish Salad

Pressure Cooker Moroccan-Style Lamb

SERVES 4

1 large onion, coarsely chopped

2 garlic cloves, finely chopped

1 pound boneless leg of lamb, trimmed and cut into ½-inch pieces

1 teaspoon cinnamon

¼ teaspoon saffron threads, crushed

1 teaspoon ground ginger

½ teaspoon salt

⅛ teaspoon cayenne

1½ cups reduced-sodium vegetable broth

12 dried apricots

1 cup frozen sliced carrots

1 red potato, scrubbed and cut into ½-inch dice (about 1 cup)

2 tablespoons chopped fresh cilantro

1 Spray a pressure cooker with nonstick spray and set over medium-high heat. Add the onion and garlic; cook, stirring, until softened, about 2 minutes. Add the lamb and cook, stirring, until lightly browned on all sides, about 2 minutes. Stir in the cinnamon, saffron, ginger, salt, and cayenne; cook, stirring, until fragrant, about 20 seconds. Stir in the broth, dried apricots, carrots, and potato.

2 Lock the lid in place and raise the heat to high. Bring the cooker to high pressure, following the manufacturer's directions. Reduce the heat and cook at high pressure for 8 minutes.

3 Place the pot in the sink and run cold water over it to bring the pressure down quickly. When the pressure indicator releases, remove the pot from the sink and unlock the lid, following the manufacturer's directions. Stir in the cilantro just before serving.

Per serving (1 cup): 275 Cal, 8 g Fat, 3 g Sat Fat, 0 g Trans Fat, 78 mg Chol, 481 mg Sod, 25 g Carb, 4 g Fib, 26 g Prot, 56 mg Calc. **PointsPlus** value: **7.**

Hunan-Style Lamb and Bell Peppers

SERVES 4

1 teaspoon cornstarch

2 teaspoons water

4 scallions, thinly sliced

4 quarter-size slices peeled fresh ginger, cut into very thin strips

2 garlic cloves, minced

¾ pound lamb loin, trimmed and cut into 2 x ¼-inch strips

3 assorted-color bell peppers, thinly sliced

1 tablespoon hoisin sauce

1 tablespoon reduced-sodium soy sauce

1 tablespoon red-wine vinegar

½ teaspoon crushed red pepper or to taste

1 teaspoon Asian (dark) sesame oil

1 Stir together the cornstarch and water in a cup until smooth.

2 Spray a nonstick wok or large deep nonstick skillet with nonstick spray and set over high heat. When a drop of water sizzles in it, add the scallions, ginger, and garlic; stir-fry until fragrant, about 20 seconds

3 Add the lamb and stir-fry until browned, about 2 minutes. Add the bell peppers and stir-fry until crisp-tender, about 2 minutes. Stir in the hoisin sauce, soy sauce, vinegar, crushed red pepper, and sesame oil; stir-fry until fragrant, about 1 minute.

4 Stir the cornstarch mixture and add to the wok; stir-fry until the sauce thickens and bubbles, about 30 seconds.

Per serving (1¼ cups): 200 Cal, 8 g Fat, 2 g Sat Fat, 0 g Trans Fat, 62 mg Chol, 271 mg Sod, 12 g Carb, 3 g Fib, 21 g Prot, 37 mg Calc. **PointsPlus** value: **5.**

◆ Filling Extra

Bulk up this stir-fry by adding 2 cups small broccoli florets along with the bell peppers in step 3.

Easy Moussaka

SERVES 6

1 large onion, chopped

2 garlic cloves, minced

1 pound ground lean lamb

2 teaspoons dried oregano

1 teaspoon cinnamon

½ teaspoon salt

¼ teaspoon black pepper

¾ cup reduced-sodium chicken broth

3 tablespoons tomato paste

12 ounces fresh linguine

2 tablespoons grated Parmesan cheese

1 Bring 3 quarts of water to a boil in a large pot over high heat.

2 Meanwhile, spray a large nonstick skillet with nonstick spray and set over medium-high heat. Add the onion and garlic; cook, stirring, until golden, about 4 minutes.

3 Add the lamb to the skillet and cook, breaking it apart with a wooden spoon, until browned, about 2 minutes. Add the oregano, cinnamon, salt, and pepper; cook until fragrant, about 15 seconds. Stir in the broth and tomato paste; bring to a boil. Reduce the heat and simmer, covered, stirring occasionally, about 10 minutes.

4 Meanwhile, add the linguine to the boiling water and cook until al dente, about 2 minutes; drain. Divide the pasta among 6 large shallow bowls; top evenly with the lamb mixture and sprinkle with the Parmesan.

Per serving (½ cup linguine, ½ cup lamb mixture, and 1 teaspoon Parmesan): 308 Cal, 8 g Fat, 2 g Sat Fat, 0 g Trans Fat, 94 mg Chol, 374 mg Sod, 35 g Carb, 3 g Fib, 24 g Prot, 56 mg Calc. *PointsPlus* value: **7.**

Easy Moussaka

Lamb Burgers with Garlicky Yogurt Sauce

SERVES 4

1¼ pounds ground lean lamb

2 scallions, chopped

1 teaspoon dried oregano

½ teaspoon salt

¼ teaspoon black pepper

¼ cup plain reduced-fat (2%) Greek-style yogurt

1 tablespoon chopped fresh mint

1 small garlic clove, minced

1 teaspoon lemon juice

4 green leaf lettuce leaves

2 tomatoes, sliced

4 small hard rolls, split

1 Spray a nonstick ridged grill pan with nonstick spray and set over medium-high heat.

2 Meanwhile, mix together the lamb, scallions, oregano, salt, and pepper in a large bowl. With damp hands, shape the mixture into 4 (½-inch-thick) patties. Place the patties on the grill pan and cook until an instant-read thermometer inserted into the side of a burger registers 160°F, about 4 minutes on each side.

3 To make the yogurt sauce, combine the yogurt, mint, garlic, and lemon juice in a small bowl. Divide the lettuce and tomatoes evenly among the bottoms of the rolls and top each with a burger. Spoon the yogurt sauce evenly on top and cover with the tops of the rolls.

Per serving (1 garnished burger): 322 Cal, 10 g Fat, 3 g Sat Fat, 1 g Trans Fat, 79 mg Chol, 583 mg Sod, 26 g Carb, 2 g Fib, 30 g Prot, 120 mg Calc. **PointsPlus** value: **9.**

Time-Saver

Use 1 teaspoon dried mint instead of the fresh.

Veal Cutlets with Lemon-Caper Sauce

SERVES 4

2 tablespoons all-purpose flour

¾ teaspoon salt

¼ teaspoon black pepper

4 (¼-pound) veal cutlets

2 tablespoons unsalted butter

⅓ cup dry white wine

2 teaspoons lemon juice

1 tablespoon capers, drained

1 tablespoon chopped fresh
   parsley

1 Combine the flour, salt, and pepper on a sheet of wax paper. Place the cutlets between pieces of plastic wrap. With a meat mallet or rolling pin, pound the cutlets to ¼-inch thickness. Coat with the seasoned flour, shaking off the excess.

2 Melt the butter in a large nonstick skillet over medium-high heat. Add the veal and cook until browned and cooked through, 2–3 minutes on each side. Transfer to a platter; keep warm.

3 Reduce the heat to medium and add the wine, lemon juice, capers, and parsley to the skillet; cook about 1 minute. Pour the sauce over the cutlets.

Per serving (1 veal cutlet and about 1½ teaspoons sauce): 183 Cal, 10 g Fat, 5 g Sat Fat, 0 g Trans Fat, 89 mg Chol, 571 mg Sod, 4 g Carb, 0 g Fib, 18 g Prot, 26 mg Calc. **PointsPlus** value: **5.**

Turkey–Green Chile Tacos

4

Chicken and Turkey Any Way You Like It

Chicken with Cremini Mushroom—Port Sauce

Cornmeal-Crusted Chicken with Nectarine-Basil Salsa

Grilled Chicken and Persimmon Salad

Chicken and Coconut Curry

Chicken, White Bean, and Arugula Salad

Stir-Fried Chicken and Mushrooms with Cellophane Noodles

New Orleans—Style Chicken

Chicken with Feta and Tomatoes

Grilled Chicken with Blood Orange Salad

Sautéed Chicken Breasts with Tomato-Caper Sauce

Greek-Style Chicken with Yogurt Sauce

Moroccan-Style Chicken Stew

Szechuan Chicken and Bok Choy Stir-Fry

Sloppy Joes Tex-Mex Style

Microwave Deviled Chicken

Chicken and Mushroom Bolognese

Sausages and Onion on Crispy Polenta

Key West—Style Roasted Chicken Salad

Chicken, Rice, and Black Bean Salad

Warm Curried Chicken Salad

Parmesan Turkey Cutlets with Arugula and Tomato

Ham and Swiss—Stuffed Turkey Rolls

Middle Eastern—Style Turkey Burgers

Turkey—Green Chile Tacos

Scallion-Ginger Meatballs

Turkey and Corn Quesadillas

Sausage and Onion Fajitas

Fresh Linguine with Sausage and Spinach

Chicken with Cremini Mushroom—Port Sauce

SERVES 4

4 (5-ounce) skinless boneless chicken breast halves

½ teaspoon salt

¼ teaspoon black pepper

2 teaspoons olive oil

1 (10-ounce) package sliced cremini mushrooms

⅓ cup ruby port wine

⅓ cup reduced-sodium chicken broth

2 teaspoons all-purpose flour

2 garlic cloves, minced

½ teaspoon dried thyme

1 Sprinkle the chicken with the salt and pepper. Heat 1 teaspoon of the oil in a large nonstick skillet over medium-high heat. Add the chicken and cook until lightly browned, about 3 minutes on each side. Transfer to a plate; set aside.

2 Add the remaining 1 teaspoon oil to the skillet. Add the mushrooms and cook, stirring, until browned, about 4 minutes.

3 Stir together the port, broth, and flour in a small bowl until smooth. Pour into the skillet. Add the garlic and thyme; cook, stirring constantly, until the sauce thickens and bubbles, about 1 minute.

4 Return the chicken to the skillet, turning to coat with the sauce. Reduce the heat and simmer, covered, until cooked through, about 3 minutes on each side.

Per serving (1 chicken breast half and generous ⅓ cup sauce): 237 Cal, 7 g Fat, 2 g Sat Fat, 0 g Trans Fat, 86 mg Chol, 423 mg Sod, 7 g Carb, 1 g Fib, 34 g Prot, 28 mg Calc. **PointsPlus** value: **6.**

◆ Filling Extra

Serve with 4 cups of cooked yellow wax or green beans seasoned with a squeeze of fresh lemon juice and a sprinkling of salt.

Chicken with Cremini Mushroom–Port Sauce

Cornmeal-Crusted Chicken with Nectarine-Basil Salsa

SERVES 4

4 large nectarines, halved, pitted and chopped

½ cup chopped fresh basil

4 teaspoons white vinegar

¾ teaspoon salt

¼ + ⅛ teaspoon black pepper

½ teaspoon dried lavender buds (optional)

2 tablespoons yellow cornmeal

4 (5-ounce) skinless boneless chicken breast halves

2 teaspoons olive oil

1 To make the salsa, combine the nectarines, basil, vinegar, ¼ teaspoon of the salt, ⅛ teaspoon of pepper, and the lavender, if using, in a serving bowl; set aside.

2 Combine the cornmeal and the remaining ½ teaspoon salt and ¼ teaspoon pepper on a sheet of wax paper. Coat the chicken with the cornmeal mixture pressing lightly so it adheres.

3 Heat the oil in a large nonstick skillet over medium-high heat. Add the chicken and cook until lightly browned and cooked through, about 5 minutes on each side. Serve with the salsa.

Per serving (1 chicken breast half and about ⅔ cup salsa): 284 Cal, 7 g Fat, 2 g Sat Fat, 0 g Trans Fat, 86 mg Chol, 520 mg Sod, 21 g Carb, 3 g Fib, 33 g Prot, 34 mg Calc. *PointsPlus* value: **6.**

Grilled Chicken and Persimmon Salad

SERVES 4

4 (5-ounce) skinless boneless chicken breast halves

1 teaspoon dried basil

½ + ⅛ teaspoon salt

¼ teaspoon black pepper

2 tablespoons apple-cider vinegar

2 tablespoons chopped white onion

1 tablespoon olive oil

1 tablespoon all-fruit strawberry spread

8 ounces mixed baby salad greens

1 Fuyu persimmon, halved and thinly sliced

1 Sprinkle the chicken with the basil, ½ teaspoon of the salt, and the pepper.

2 Spray a nonstick ridged grill pan with nonstick spray and set over medium-high heat. Add the chicken and cook until browned and cooked through, about 3 minutes on each side.

3 Meanwhile, whisk together the vinegar, onion, oil, strawberry spread, and the remaining ⅛ teaspoon salt in a serving bowl. Add the salad greens and toss to coat evenly.

4 Cut the chicken breasts on the diagonal into thin slices. Add the chicken and persimmon to the salad and toss to mix well.

Per serving (about 2 cups): 259 Cal, 8 g Fat, 2 g Sat Fat, 0 g Trans Fat, 86 mg Chol, 464 mg Sod, 13 g Carb, 3 g Fib, 32 g Prot, 53 mg Calc. *PointsPlus* value: **6.**

Chicken and Coconut Curry

SERVES 4

¾ pound skinless boneless chicken breast halves, cut into 1½-inch chunks

¼ teaspoon salt

1 teaspoon canola oil

1 red bell pepper, cut into strips

6 scallions, chopped

2½ teaspoons Thai red curry paste

2 teaspoons sugar

1 teaspoon ground cumin

½ teaspoon ground coriander

1 (14-ounce) can light coconut milk

1 (12-ounce) bag cauliflower florets

1 (6-ounce) bag matchstick-cut carrots

1 Sprinkle the chicken with the salt. Heat ½ teaspoon of the oil in a large nonstick skillet over medium-high heat. Add the chicken and cook, turning occasionally, until browned and cooked through, about 5 minutes. Transfer to a plate; set aside.

2 Add the remaining ½ teaspoon oil to the skillet. Add the bell pepper and scallions; cook, stirring, until the scallions turn bright green, about 1 minute. Add the curry paste, sugar, cumin, and coriander; cook, stirring constantly, about 1 minute. Stir in the coconut milk, cauliflower, and carrots; bring to a boil. Reduce the heat and simmer, covered, stirring occasionally, until the vegetables are tender, about 6 minutes longer.

3 Return the chicken to the skillet and cook until heated through, about 1 minute.

Per serving (1½ cups): 340 Cal, 10 g Fat, 4 g Sat Fat, 0 g Trans Fat, 51 mg Chol, 292 mg Sod, 40 g Carb, 8 g Fib, 25 g Prot, 82 mg Calc. **PointsPlus** value: **6.**

WEIGHT WATCHERS IN 20 MINUTES

Chicken and Coconut Curry

Chicken, White Bean, and Arugula Salad

SERVES 4

1 (15½-ounce) can cannellini (white kidney) beans, rinsed and drained

1 tomato, chopped

1 small onion, thinly sliced

¼ cup lightly packed flat-leaf parsley leaves

8 pimiento-stuffed green olives, chopped

5 tablespoons fat-free Italian dressing

4 (5-ounce) skinless boneless chicken breast halves

1 (5-ounce) bag baby arugula, trimmed

1 Combine the beans, tomato, onion, parsley, and olives in a medium bowl. Drizzle with 3 tablespoons of the dressing and toss to coat evenly; set aside.

2 Spray a ridged grill pan with olive oil nonstick spray and set over medium-high heat. Brush the chicken with the remaining 2 tablespoons dressing. Place on the grill pan and cook until browned and cooked through, about 5 minutes on each side. Cut the chicken breasts on the diagonal into thin slices.

3 Divide the arugula evenly among 4 plates and top each serving with 1 sliced chicken breast. Spoon about ½ cup of the cannellini bean mixture on top of each serving.

Per serving (generous 2 cups): 300 Cal, 6 g Fat, 2 g Sat Fat, 0 g Trans Fat, 86 mg Chol, 537 mg Sod, 22 g Carb, 6 g Fib, 39 g Prot, 74 mg Calc. ***PointsPlus*** value: **7.**

Stir-Fried Chicken and Mushrooms with Cellophane Noodles

SERVES 4

6 ounces cellophane noodles

1 tablespoon peanut oil

2 garlic cloves, minced

1 red bell pepper, cut into thin strips

¼ pound green beans, trimmed and halved (about 1 cup)

8 shiitake mushrooms, stemmed, caps sliced

6 scallions, cut into 2-inch lengths

¾ pound skinless boneless chicken breast halves, cut on the diagonal into strips

½ teaspoon salt

¼ teaspoon black pepper

1 tablespoon reduced-sodium soy sauce

1   Put the noodles in a large bowl and add hot water to cover. Let stand until softened, about 10 minutes; drain. Transfer to a platter; keep warm.

2   Meanwhile, heat the oil in a nonstick wok or large deep nonstick skillet over high heat. When a drop of water sizzles in the pan, add the garlic and stir-fry until fragrant, about 30 seconds. Add the bell pepper, green beans, mushrooms, and scallions; stir-fry until the green beans are crisp-tender, about 3 minutes. Transfer to a bowl; keep warm.

3   Sprinkle the chicken with the salt and pepper. Add to the wok and stir-fry, adding 1 tablespoon of water to prevent sticking if necessary, until lightly browned and cooked through, about 4 minutes. Return the vegetables to the wok; add the soy sauce and stir-fry until the vegetables are heated through, about 2 minutes. Spoon over the noodles.

Per serving (2 cups): 316 Cal, 6 g Fat, 1 g Sat Fat, 0 g Trans Fat, 52 mg Chol, 484 mg Sod, 44 g Carb, 3 g Fib, 22 g Prot, 51 mg Calc. **PointsPlus** value: **8.**

⏱ Time-Saver

Look for bags of trimmed fresh green beans in the produce section of the supermarket.

New Orleans—Style Chicken

SERVES 4

WEIGHT WATCHERS IN 20 MINUTES

2 tablespoons all-purpose flour

1¼ teaspoons Cajun seasoning

¾ pound skinless boneless chicken breast halves, cut into strips

2 teaspoons canola oil

1½ cups frozen corn kernels, thawed

1½ cups frozen cut okra, thawed

2 large plum tomatoes, chopped

2 garlic cloves, minced

½ cup fat-free half-and-half

¼ teaspoon salt

3 scallions, sliced

1 Combine the flour and ½ teaspoon of the Cajun seasoning in a large zip-close plastic bag. Add the chicken; seal the bag and shake to coat the chicken evenly.

2 Heat 1½ teaspoons of the oil in a large nonstick skillet over medium-high heat. Add the chicken and cook, turning, until lightly browned and cooked through, about 4 minutes. Transfer the chicken to a plate; set aside.

3 Add the remaining ½ teaspoon oil to the skillet. Add the corn, okra, tomato, and garlic; cook, stirring occasionally, until almost tender, about 2 minutes. Add the half-and-half, the remaining ¾ teaspoon Cajun seasoning and the salt; bring to a simmer and cook until slightly thickened, about 1 minute.

4 Return the chicken to the skillet and cook, stirring occasionally, until heated through, about 2 minutes. Transfer to a serving bowl and sprinkle with the scallions.

Per serving (1¼ cups): 234 Cal, 6 g Fat, 1 g Sat Fat, 0 g Trans Fat, 53 mg Chol, 412 mg Sod, 23 g Carb, 4 g Fib, 23 g Prot, 120 mg Calc. *PointsPlus* value: **6.**

Chicken with Feta and Tomatoes

SERVES 4

4 (3-ounce) chicken breast
cutlets

½ teaspoon salt

½ teaspoon black pepper

1½ teaspoons olive oil

1 pint grape tomatoes

1 tablespoon finely chopped
fresh oregano

2 garlic cloves, minced

½ cup diced cucumber

¼ cup crumbled reduced-fat feta
cheese

1 Sprinkle the chicken with ¼ teaspoon of the salt and ¼ teaspoon of the pepper. Heat 1 teaspoon of the oil in a large nonstick skillet over medium-high heat. Add the chicken and cook until browned and cooked through, about 2 minutes on each side. Transfer to a platter; keep warm.

2 Add the remaining ½ teaspoon oil to the skillet; add the tomatoes, oregano, garlic, and the remaining ¼ teaspoon salt and ¼ teaspoon pepper. Cook, stirring, until the tomatoes are softened, about 3 minutes. Spoon the sauce over the chicken and sprinkle with the cucumber and feta.

Per serving (1 chicken cutlet, ¼ cup sauce, 2 tablespoons cucumber, and 1 tablespoon feta): 163 Cal, 6 g Fat, 2 g Sat Fat, 0 g Trans Fat, 55 mg Chol, 481 mg Sod, 6 g Carb, 2 g Fib, 21 g Prot, 74 mg Calc. **PointsPlus** value: **3.**

◆ Filling Extra

Accompany this flavorful Greek-inspired dish with whole wheat couscous tossed with 1 or 2 thinly sliced scallions and snipped fresh dill (½ cup cooked whole wheat couscous per serving will increase the **PointsPlus** value by **3**).

Grilled Chicken with Blood Orange Salad

SERVES 4

½ cup blood orange or regular orange juice

2 tablespoons lemon juice

2 teaspoons chopped fresh thyme

2 garlic cloves, minced

1 tablespoon olive oil

¾ teaspoon salt

¼ teaspoon black pepper

4 (¼-pound) chicken breast cutlets

1 cucumber, peeled, halved, and sliced

1 blood orange or regular orange, peeled and sectioned

1 orange bell pepper, cut into strips

¼ cup pitted kalamata olives

1 Whisk together the orange juice, lemon juice, thyme, garlic, oil, salt, and black pepper in a small bowl. Pour half of the mixture into a medium bowl and add the chicken, turning to coat.

2 Spray a nonstick ridged grill pan with nonstick spray and set over medium-high heat. Remove the chicken from the marinade; discard the marinade. Place the chicken on the grill pan and cook until cooked through, about 3 minutes on each side.

3 Meanwhile, put the cucumber, orange, bell pepper, and olives in a serving bowl; drizzle with the remaining orange juice mixture and toss to coat evenly. Serve with the chicken.

Per serving (1 chicken cutlet and ⅔ cup salad): 208 Cal, 7 g Fat, 1 g Sat Fat, 0 g Trans Fat, 68 mg Chol, 416 mg Sod, 10 g Carb, 2 g Fib, 26 g Prot, 46 mg Calc. **PointsPlus** value: **5.**

⏱ Time-Saver

Substitute ½ teaspoon dried thyme for the fresh.

Grilled Chicken with Blood Orange Salad

Sautéed Chicken Breasts with Tomato-Caper Sauce

SERVES 4

4 (¼-pound) chicken breast cutlets

½ teaspoon salt

¼ teaspoon black pepper

2 teaspoons olive oil

½ small onion, chopped

2 garlic cloves, minced

¼ cup dry red wine

1 (14½-ounce) can diced tomatoes

5 pitted brine-cured kalamata olives, halved

1 tablespoon capers, drained

1 teaspoon dried thyme

1 Sprinkle the chicken with the salt and pepper. Heat the oil in a large nonstick skillet over medium-high heat. Add the chicken and cook until browned and cooked through, about 2 minutes on each side; transfer to a plate. Set aside.

2 Add the onion and garlic to the skillet; cook until softened, about 1 minute. Add the wine and cook about 2 minutes. Add the tomatoes with their juice, the olives, capers, and thyme. Reduce the heat and simmer until the sauce thickens slightly, about 5 minutes longer.

3 Return the chicken to the skillet and cook until heated through, about 1 minute.

Per serving (1 chicken cutlet and about ⅓ cup sauce): 186 Cal, 4 g Fat, 1 g Sat Fat, 0 g Trans Fat, 66 mg Chol, 878 mg Sod, 8 g Carb, 1 g Fib, 28 g Prot, 34 mg Calc. *PointsPlus* value: **5.**

Greek-Style Chicken with Yogurt Sauce

SERVES 4

¾ cup plain fat-free yogurt

⅓ cup shredded peeled cucumber

2 teaspoons lemon juice

2 garlic cloves, minced

½ teaspoon salt

½ teaspoon black pepper

2 cups chopped romaine lettuce

1 tomato, chopped

2 scallions, sliced

8 chicken tenders (about ¾ pound)

1 teaspoon dried oregano

2 teaspoons olive oil

2 cups hot cooked quick-cooking brown rice

1 Combine the yogurt, cucumber, lemon juice, half of the garlic, ¼ teaspoon of the salt, and ¼ teaspoon of the pepper in a small bowl; set aside. Toss together the lettuce, tomato, and scallions in a medium bowl; set aside.

2 Toss together the chicken, the remaining garlic, the oregano, and the remaining ¼ teaspoon salt and ¼ teaspoon pepper in a medium bowl.

3 Heat the oil in a large nonstick skillet over medium-high heat. Add the chicken and cook until browned and cooked through, about 2 minutes on each side.

4 Place ½ cup of the rice on each of 4 plates; top each serving with one-fourth of the lettuce mixture, 2 chicken tenders, and ¼ cup of the yogurt sauce.

Per serving (1 plate): 282 Cal, 6 g Fat, 1 g Sat Fat, 0 g Trans Fat, 52 mg Chol, 658 mg Sod, 31 g Carb, 4 g Fib, 25 g Prot, 138 mg Calc. **PointsPlus** value: **6.**

⏱ Time-Saver

Microwave an 8.8-ounce package of shelf-stable cooked brown rice according to the package directions. It will be ready in 90 seconds.

Moroccan-Style Chicken Stew

SERVES 4

1 pound chicken tenders, cut into 1-inch pieces

¾ teaspoon salt

¼ teaspoon black pepper

1 tablespoon olive oil

1 onion, sliced

2 garlic cloves, minced

1 teaspoon ground cumin

½ teaspoon cinnamon

1 (14½-ounce) can reduced-sodium chicken broth

1 (12-ounce) package frozen squash puree, thawed

1 cup frozen corn kernels

1 Season the chicken with ½ teaspoon of the salt and ⅛ teaspoon of the pepper. Heat the oil in a large nonstick skillet over medium-high heat. Add the chicken and cook, stirring, until cooked through, about 4 minutes. Add the onion, garlic, cumin, and cinnamon; cook until fragrant, about 1 minute longer.

2 Add the broth, squash, corn, and the remaining ¼ teaspoon salt and ⅛ teaspoon pepper to the skillet. Cook, stirring, until the corn is tender and the sauce is heated through, about 5 minutes.

Per serving (1¼ cups): 260 Cal, 8 g Fat, 1 g Sat Fat, 0 g Trans Fat, 68 mg Chol, 745 mg Sod, 20 g Carb, 4 g Fib, 29 g Prot, 62 mg Calc. **PointsPlus** value: **6.**

Szechuan Chicken and Bok Choy Stir-Fry

SERVES 4

1 pound skinless boneless chicken thighs, trimmed and cut into 1-inch chunks

2 tablespoons sesame seeds

2 teaspoons canola oil

1 pound baby bok choy, quartered lengthwise

1 yellow bell pepper, cut into thin strips

½ pound snow peas, trimmed

2 scallions, cut into 1½-inch lengths

⅓ cup Szechuan stir-fry sauce

⅓ cup orange juice

2 cups hot cooked quick-cooking brown rice

1 Sprinkle the chicken with the sesame seeds. Heat 1 teaspoon of the oil in a nonstick wok or large deep nonstick skillet over medium-high heat. When a drop of water sizzles in it, add the chicken and stir-fry just until cooked through, about 6 minutes. Transfer to a plate; set aside.

2 Add the remaining 1 teaspoon oil to the wok and set over high heat. Add the bok choy, bell pepper, snow peas, and scallions; stir-fry until the bok choy is crisp-tender, 4–5 minutes. Return the chicken to the wok and add the stir-fry sauce and orange juice; stir-fry until heated through, about 1 minute. Serve with the rice.

Per serving (1 ¾ cups chicken mixture and ½ cup rice): 394 Cal, 15 g Fat, 4 g Sat Fat, 0 g Trans Fat, 71 mg Chol, 866 mg Sod, 33 g Carb, 6 g Fib, 32 g Prot, 165 mg Calc. **PointsPlus** value: **10.**

⏱ Time-Saver

Rather than spending time trimming the fat from the chicken thighs, substitute the same amount of chicken tenders, cut them into 1-inch pieces, and reduce the cooking time in step 1 to about 4 minutes.

Sloppy Joes Tex-Mex Style

SERVES 4

2 teaspoons olive oil

1 pound ground skinless chicken breast

1 teaspoon taco or Mexican seasoning

¼ teaspoon salt

¼ teaspoon black pepper

1½ cups prepared black bean and corn salsa

¼ cup fat-free sour cream

1 tablespoon lime juice

4 (7-inch) whole-wheat tortillas, warmed

2 tablespoons coarsely chopped fresh cilantro

1 scallion, chopped

1 Heat the oil in a large nonstick skillet over medium-high heat. Add the chicken, taco seasoning, salt, and pepper; cook, breaking the chicken apart with a wooden spoon, until no longer pink, about 6 minutes. Stir in the salsa and cook until heated through, about 3 minutes longer. Remove the skillet from the heat and set aside.

2 Combine the sour cream and lime juice in a small bowl.

3 Place 1 warm tortilla on each of 4 plates. Spoon about ¾ cup of the chicken mixture onto each tortilla; top with about 1½ tablespoons of the sour cream mixture. Sprinkle with the cilantro and scallion.

Per serving (1 plate): 299 Cal, 7 g Fat, 2 g Sat Fat, 0 g Trans Fat, 70 mg Chol, 567 mg Sod, 29 g Carb, 6 g Fib, 31 g Prot, 69 mg Calc. **PointsPlus** value: **7.**

⏱ Time-Saver

To make another quick dinner later in the week, prepare a double amount of the chicken mixture. Transfer half to an airtight container, then cover and refrigerate up to 3 days.

Sloppy Joes Tex-Mex Style

Microwave Deviled Chicken

SERVES 4

½ cup plain dried bread crumbs

¼ teaspoon dried thyme

¼ teaspoon salt

¼ teaspoon black pepper

3 tablespoons Dijon mustard

1 teaspoon hot pepper sauce

1 teaspoon Worcestershire sauce

1 teaspoon honey

4 skinless chicken thighs
(1½ pounds), trimmed

1 Spray a microwavable 2-quart shallow baking dish with nonstick spray.

2 Combine the bread crumbs, thyme, salt, and pepper on a sheet of wax paper. Combine the mustard, pepper sauce, Worcestershire sauce, and honey in a medium bowl; add the chicken and toss to coat evenly. Coat the thighs, one at a time, with the bread crumbs, pressing lightly so they adhere. Place the chicken in the baking dish in a single layer and lightly spray with nonstick spray.

3 Cover the chicken with wax paper and microwave on High 8 minutes. Uncover and microwave on High until the chicken is cooked through, about 2 minutes longer. Let stand about 3 minutes before serving.

Per serving (1 chicken thigh): 251 Cal, 10 g Fat, 3 g Sat Fat, 0 g Trans Fat, 69 mg Chol, 609 mg Sod, 12 g Carb, 1 g Fib, 26 g Prot, 60 mg Calc. *PointsPlus* value: **7.**

◆ Filling Extra

This comfort-food specialty pairs well with polenta (½ cup cooked polenta per serving will increase the *PointsPlus* value by **3**).

Chicken and Mushroom Bolognese

SERVES 4

1 (9-ounce) package fresh
fettuccine

4 teaspoons olive oil

1 onion, finely chopped

1 small carrot, chopped

1 small celery stalk, chopped

2 garlic cloves, minced

½ pound ground skinless
chicken breast

1 (10-ounce) package sliced
white mushrooms

½ teaspoon salt

½ teaspoon black pepper

1 cup prepared fat-free marinara
sauce

1 Cook the fettuccine according to the package directions. Drain, reserving ½ cup of the water.

2 Meanwhile, heat the oil in a large nonstick skillet over medium-high heat. Add the onion, carrot, celery, and garlic; cook, stirring, until the onion is golden, about 4 minutes. Add the chicken and cook, breaking it apart with a wooden spoon, until no longer pink, about 3 minutes. Add the mushrooms, salt, and pepper; cook, stirring occasionally, about 2 minutes. Add the marinara sauce and bring to a simmer.

3 Add the pasta to the Bolognese sauce and toss, adding enough of the reserved cooking water to moisten the sauce, if needed.

Per serving (1½ cups): 329 Cal, 8 g Fat, 2 g Sat Fat, 0 g Trans Fat, 75 mg Chol, 682 mg Sod, 42 g Carb, 4 g Fib, 22 g Prot, 45 mg Calc. **PointsPlus** value: **8.**

⏱ Time-Saver

Quarter the onion, carrot, and celery stalk, place in a food processor, and pulse until chopped.

Sausages and Onion on Crispy Polenta

SERVES 4

1 (16-ounce) tube fat-free
  polenta, cut into 12 slices

1 large red bell pepper, cut into
  strips

1 large onion, sliced

½ pound fully cooked
  sun-dried tomato and chicken
  sausages, cut into 1-inch slices

1 teaspoon Italian seasoning

1 cup prepared fat-free marinara
  sauce

⅓ cup water

6 pitted kalamata olives, sliced

2 tablespoons coarsely chopped
  flat-leaf parsley

1 Spray a large nonstick ridged grill pan with nonstick spray and set over high heat. Arrange the polenta slices on the pan and lightly spray with nonstick spray. Cook until golden, about 5 minutes on each side.

2 Meanwhile, spray a large nonstick skillet with nonstick spray and set over medium-high heat. Add the bell pepper and onion; cook, stirring, until softened, about 3 minutes. Stir in the sausages and Italian seasoning; cook until the sausages are lightly browned, about 2 minutes. Add the remaining ingredients; bring to a boil. Reduce the heat and simmer until heated through, about 1 minute longer. Transfer the polenta to a platter and top with the sausage mixture.

Per serving (3 slices polenta and ¾ cup sausage mixture): 238 Cal, 9 g Fat, 2 g Sat Fat, 0 g Trans Fat, 33 mg Chol, 900 mg Sod, 28 g Carb, 3 g Fib, 13 g Prot, 49 mg Calc. *PointsPlus* value: **7.**

Sausages and Onion on Crispy Polenta

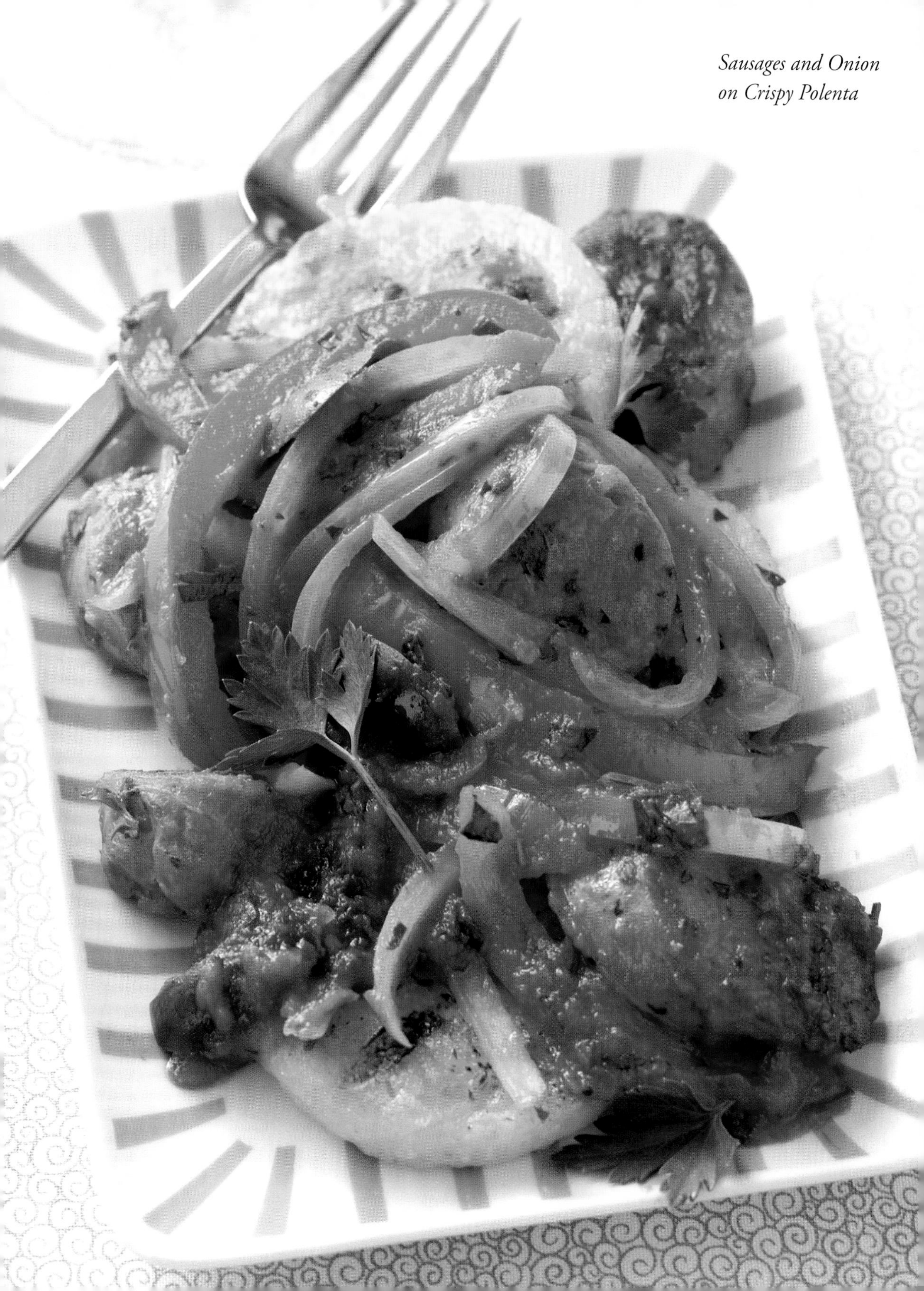

Key West–Style Roasted Chicken Salad

SERVES 4

3 tablespoons key lime juice

2 tablespoons taco sauce

2 teaspoons olive oil

¾ teaspoon salt

3 cups sliced deli roast chicken breast

1 bunch arugula, torn

1 cup grape tomatoes

½ small red onion, thinly sliced

½ cup chopped fresh cilantro

Whisk together the lime juice, taco sauce, oil, and salt in a serving bowl. Add the remaining ingredients and toss to coat evenly.

Per serving (generous 1½ cups): 218 Cal, 7 g Fat, 2 g Sat Fat, 0 Trans Fat, 86 mg Chol, 666 mg Sod, 5 g Carb, 1 g Fib, 33 g Prot, 72 mg Calc. **PointsPlus** value: **5.**

⏱ Time-Saver

Get a head start: Combine the lime juice, taco sauce, oil, and salt in a small covered jar. Refrigerate up to 2 days ahead.

Chicken, Rice, and Black Bean Salad

SERVES 6

- 2 tablespoons lime juice
- 1 tablespoon olive oil
- 1 tablespoon chili powder
- ½ teaspoon ground cumin
- ½ teaspoon salt
- ¼ teaspoon sugar
- 2 cups cubed cooked chicken breast
- 3 cups hot cooked quick-cooking white rice
- 1 (15-ounce) can black beans, rinsed and drained
- ½ cup chopped red bell pepper
- 4 scallions, sliced
- ⅓ cup coarsely chopped fresh cilantro

Whisk together the lime juice, oil, chili powder, cumin, salt, and sugar in a serving bowl. Add the remaining ingredients and toss to combine and coat evenly with the dressing.

Per serving (scant 1 ⅓ cups): 275 Cal, 5 g Fat, 1 g Sat Fat, 0 g Trans Fat, 38 mg Chol, 735 mg Sod, 36 g Carb, 7 g Fib, 21 g Prot, 69 mg Calc. **PointsPlus** value: **6.**

◆ *Filling Extra*

Serve this salad over a bed of dark leafy greens, such as a 5-ounce bag of baby arugula or spinach.

153

Warm Curried Chicken Salad

SERVES 6

1½ cups water

1¼ teaspoons curry powder

¾ teaspoon salt

1 cup whole-wheat couscous

1 (15½-ounce) can chickpeas, rinsed and drained

1 cup shredded cooked chicken breast

1 Granny Smith apple, halved, cored, and cut into wedges

1 small red bell pepper, cut into thin strips

½ small red onion, thinly sliced

3 tablespoons lemon juice

2 teaspoons olive oil

6 cups torn romaine lettuce

1 Combine the water, 1 teaspoon of the curry powder, and ½ teaspoon of the salt in a small saucepan and bring to a boil over medium-high heat; add the couscous. Cover the pot and remove from the heat. Let stand 5 minutes, then fluff with a fork; set aside.

2 Combine the chickpeas, chicken, apple, bell pepper, onion, lemon juice, oil, and the remaining ¼ teaspoon curry powder and ¼ teaspoon salt in a large bowl. Add the couscous and mix well. Divide the lettuce among 6 plates and top each serving evenly with the chicken salad.

Per serving (generous 2 cups): 231 Cal, 5 g Fat, 1 g Sat Fat, 0 g Trans Fat, 19 mg Chol, 429 mg Sod, 35 g Carb, 8 g Fib, 15 g Prot, 64 mg Calc. **PointsPlus** value: **5.**

Warm Curried Chicken Salad

Parmesan Turkey Cutlets with Arugula and Tomato

SERVES 4

1 pint cherry tomatoes, halved

½ teaspoon salt

1 egg white

3 tablespoons yellow cornmeal

2 tablespoons grated Parmesan cheese

1 teaspoon garlic and herb seasoning

4 (¼-pound) turkey breast cutlets

4 teaspoons olive oil

1 bunch arugula, trimmed

1 Toss together the tomatoes and ¼ teaspoon of the salt in a medium bowl; set aside.

2 Lightly beat the egg white in a large shallow bowl or pie plate. Combine the cornmeal, Parmesan, garlic and herb seasoning, and the remaining ¼ teaspoon salt on a sheet of wax paper. Dip each slice of turkey into the egg mixture, then coat with the cornmeal mixture, pressing lightly so it adheres.

3 Heat the oil in a large nonstick skillet over medium-high heat. Add the turkey and cook until browned and cooked through, about 3 minutes on each side. Transfer to a platter.

4 Add the tomatoes and arugula to the skillet; cook, stirring, just until the arugula wilts slightly, about 1 minute. Serve alongside the cutlets.

Per serving (1 turkey cutlet and about ½ cup tomato-arugula mixture): 224 Cal, 7 g Fat, 2 g Sat Fat, 0 g Trans Fat, 77 mg Chol, 423 mg Sod, 10 g Carb, 2 g Fib, 30 g Prot, 63 mg Calc. *PointsPlus* value: **5.**

Time-Saver

Instead of trimming the arugula, substitute 2 cups lightly packed prewashed baby arugula or baby spinach.

Ham and Swiss—Stuffed Turkey Rolls

SERVES 4

4 (¼-pound) turkey breast cutlets

¼ teaspoon black pepper

4 (1-ounce) slices reduced-sodium black forest ham

2 (1-ounce) slices reduced-fat Swiss cheese, halved

3 tablespoons plain dried bread crumbs

1 teaspoon dried thyme

1 tablespoon reduced-fat mayonnaise

¼ cup dry white wine

¼ cup reduced-sodium chicken broth

1 teaspoon butter

1 Sprinkle the turkey with the pepper and top each cutlet with 1 slice of ham and ½ slice of Swiss cheese. Roll up, jelly-roll style; secure each roll with one or two toothpicks.

2 Combine the bread crumbs and thyme on a sheet of wax paper. Brush the turkey rolls with the mayonnaise and coat with the crumbs, pressing lightly so they adhere.

3 Spray a large nonstick skillet with nonstick spray and set over medium-high heat. Add the turkey rolls and cook until browned on all sides, about 5 minutes. Add the wine, broth, and butter; bring to a boil. Reduce the heat and simmer, covered, until the turkey is cooked through and the sauce thickens slightly, about 5 minutes longer.

Per serving (1 turkey roll): 146 Cal, 7 g Fat, 3 g Sat Fat, 0 g Trans Fat, 41 mg Chol, 420 mg Sod, 5 g Carb, 0 g Fib, 16 g Prot, 116 mg Calc. **PointsPlus** value: **4.**

◈ Filling Extra

Serve these savory turkey rolls with easy-to-prepare microwave-baked potatoes. A ½ large (5 ½-ounce) baked potato for each serving will increase the **PointsPlus** value by **4.**

Middle Eastern—Style Turkey Burgers

SERVES 4

1 pound ground skinless turkey breast

1 egg white

½ small onion, grated

¼ cup pine nuts, toasted and cooled

2 teaspoons olive oil

½ teaspoon ground cumin

½ teaspoon paprika

½ teaspoon salt

¼ teaspoon ground allspice

¼ teaspoon crushed red pepper

4 (7-inch) whole-wheat pitas, warmed

1 large tomato, cut into 8 slices

1 Spray the rack of a broiler pan with nonstick spray and preheat the broiler.

2 Mix together the turkey, egg white, onion, pine nuts, oil, cumin, paprika, salt, allspice, and crushed red pepper until well combined. With damp hands, shape the mixture into 4 (½-inch-thick) patties.

3 Place the patties on the broiler rack and broil 4 inches from the heat until an instant-read thermometer inserted into the side of a burger registers 165°F, 5–6 minutes on each side.

4 Cut off the top third of each pita (save for another use, if desired). Stuff each pita with 2 tomato slices and a burger.

Per serving (1 garnished burger): 356 Cal, 9 g Fat, 2 g Sat Fat, 0 g Trans Fat, 75 mg Chol, 653 mg Sod, 35 g Carb, 6 g Fib, 35 g Prot, 36 mg Calc. *PointsPlus* value: **9.**

⏱ *Time-Saver*

To warm the pitas in a flash, stack them on a paper towel and microwave on High about 30 seconds.

Turkey—Green Chile Tacos

SERVES 6

⅔ cup light sour cream

2 tablespoons canned diced mild green chiles, drained

2 tablespoons chopped fresh cilantro

1 teaspoon taco or Mexican seasoning

¼ teaspoon salt

12 taco shells, warmed

4 cups cubed cooked turkey breast

¾ cup shredded reduced-fat sharp cheddar cheese

1 cup thinly sliced romaine lettuce leaves

2 tomatoes, chopped

1 Combine the sour cream, chiles, cilantro, taco seasoning, and salt in a small bowl; set aside.

2 Fill each taco shell with ⅓ cup of the turkey, 1 tablespoon of the cheddar, generous 1 tablespoon of the lettuce, and about 3 tablespoons of the tomato; top with about 1 tablespoon of the sour cream mixture.

Per serving (2 tacos): 374 Cal, 14 g Fat, 6 g Sat Fat, 0 g Trans Fat, 101 mg Chol, 381 mg Sod, 28 g Carb, 3 g Fib, 35 g Prot, 269 mg Calc. **PointsPlus** value: **9.**

◆ *Filling Extra*

Slice a few extra lettuce leaves and chop another couple of tomatoes to serve with the tacos.

Scallion-Ginger Meatballs

SERVES 4

1 pound ground skinless turkey breast

3 tablespoons teriyaki sauce

3 scallions, finely chopped

2 teaspoons grated peeled fresh ginger

2 garlic cloves, minced

2 teaspoons canola oil

¼ cup hoisin sauce

2 tablespoons dry sherry or water

1 pound baby bok choy, quartered lengthwise

½ red bell pepper, cut into thin strips

2 tablespoons water

2 teaspoons sesame seeds

1 Combine the turkey, 2 tablespoons of the teriyaki sauce, the scallions, ginger, and garlic in a large bowl. With damp hands, form the mixture into 12 meatballs.

2 Heat the oil in a large nonstick skillet over medium-high heat. Add the meatballs and cook, partially covered, turning occasionally, until browned and cooked through, about 12 minutes. Transfer to a serving bowl; keep warm.

3 Add the hoisin sauce, sherry, and the remaining 1 tablespoon teriyaki sauce to the skillet; cook, scraping up any browned bits from the bottom of the pan. Cook, stirring, until slightly thickened, about 1 minute.

4 Meanwhile, combine the bok choy, bell pepper, and water in a medium nonstick skillet. Cook, covered, until tender, about 5 minutes; drain.

5 Add the meatballs and bok choy–mixture to the sauce, turning to coat the meatballs. Cook until heated through, about 1 minute longer. Serve sprinkled with the sesame seeds.

Per serving (3 meatballs, about ⅔ cup vegetables, and 1½ tablespoons sauce): 231 Cal, 5 g Fat, 1 g Sat Fat, 0 g Trans Fat, 76 mg Chol, 903 mg Sod, 16 g Carb, 2 g Fib, 30 g Prot, 155 mg Calc. *PointsPlus* value: **5.**

⏱ Time-Saver

Substitute 3 cups packaged fresh broccoli or cauliflower florets for the bok choy.

Turkey and Corn Quesadillas

SERVES 4

- 4 (7-inch) whole-wheat tortillas
- 1 cup shredded reduced-fat cheddar cheese
- 1 cup shredded cooked turkey breast
- 1 (8¾-ounce) can corn kernels, drained
- 1 (7-ounce) jar roasted red pepper, drained and chopped
- 4 tablespoons chopped fresh cilantro
- ¼ cup fat-free sour cream
- ¼ cup prepared salsa

1 Top half of each tortilla with ¼ cup of the cheddar, ¼ cup of the turkey, one-fourth of the corn, one-fourth of the roasted peppers, and 1 tablespoon of the cilantro. Fold the unfilled tortilla half over the filling, lightly pressing down.

2 Spray a large nonstick skillet with nonstick spray and set over medium heat. Add 2 of the quesadillas and cook until the tortillas are crisp and the cheese begins to melt, about 1½ minutes on each side. Repeat with the remaining 2 quesadillas.

3 Cut each quesadilla in half and transfer to a platter. Serve with the sour cream and salsa.

Per serving (2 wedges, 1 tablespoon sour cream, and 1 tablespoon salsa): 224 Cal, 4 g Fat, 2 g Sat Fat, 0 g Trans Fat, 36 mg Chol, 893 mg Sod, 28 g Carb, 4 g Fib, 22 g Prot, 243 mg Calc. **PointsPlus** value: **6.**

⏱ Time-Saver

Use a griddle instead of a skillet and you can cook all the quesadillas at the same time.

Sausage and Onion Fajitas

SERVES 4

1 teaspoon canola oil

½ pound Italian-style turkey
sausages, cut into ½-inch
slices

1 red bell pepper, cut into thin
strips

1 green bell pepper, cut into thin
strips

1 large red onion, thinly sliced

4 (8-inch) reduced-fat flour
tortillas, warmed

1 Heat the oil in a large nonstick skillet over
medium heat. Add the sausage and cook, stirring,
until browned, about 5 minutes. Add the bell
peppers and onion; cook, stirring, until tender,
about 8 minutes.

2 Spoon the sausage mixture evenly onto
the center of each tortilla and roll up to enclose
the filling.

Per serving (1 fajita): 241 Cal, 7 g Fat, 1 g Sat Fat,
0 g Trans Fat, 52 mg Chol, 735 mg Sod, 28 g Carb,
5 g Fib, 18 g Prot, 100 mg Calc. *PointsPlus* value: **6.**

◆ *Filling Extra*

Make these fajitas even more delicious by sprinkling
shredded fat-free mozzarella and dried oregano
over the sausage mixture (¼ cup shredded fat-free
mozzarella cheese per serving will increase the
PointsPlus value by **1**).

Fresh Linguine with Sausage and Spinach

SERVES 4

1 (9-ounce) package fresh
   linguine

2 teaspoons olive oil

½ pound hot Italian turkey
   sausages, casings removed

2 tablespoons pine nuts

1 garlic clove, minced

1 (9-ounce) bag baby spinach

1 Cook the linguine according to the package directions. Drain, reserving ½ cup of the water.

2 Meanwhile, heat the oil in a large nonstick skillet over medium-high heat. Add the sausage and cook, breaking it up with a wooden spoon, until browned, about 5 minutes. Transfer to a plate and set aside.

3 Add the pine nuts and garlic to the skillet; cook, stirring frequently until the nuts are lightly browned, about 2 minutes; add to the sausage. Add the spinach to the skillet and cook, stirring, just until wilted, about 3 minutes.

4 Return the sausage and pine nuts to the skillet; cook, stirring, until heated through, about 2 minutes. Add the pasta and reserved cooking water; cook, stirring, until heated through, about 1 minute.

Per serving (1½ cups): 333 Cal, 13 g Fat, 3 g Sat Fat, 0 g Trans Fat, 74 mg Chol, 418 mg Sod, 36 g Carb, 4 g Fib, 18 g Prot, 89 mg Calc. **PointsPlus** value: **9.**

⏱ Time-Saver

To boil water for pasta in a hurry, start with hot tap water and cover the pot.

Ham-Wrapped Flounder with
Spinach Stuffing

5

Fresh, Fast Fish

Salmon Cakes with
Red Pepper Mayonnaise

Soy and Ginger—Marinated Salmon

Orange and Lime—Marinated Halibut

Swordfish with Asian Flavors

Mediterranean-Style Swordfish

Sesame-Crusted Tuna Steaks

Bayou-Style Tuna with
Roasted Pepper Sauce

Greek-Style Cod Fillets

Cod with Tomato-Fennel Salsa

Microwave Creole Cod

Mahimahi with Shallot-Mustard Sauce

Snapper with Easy Pesto Sauce

Striped Bass with Cherry
Tomato—Caper Sauce

Sea Bass with Green Sauce

Parmesan and Potato—Crusted Flounder
with Tomato-Cilantro Sauce

Ham-Wrapped Flounder
with Spinach Stuffing

Orange Roughy with
Spicy Tomato Sauce

Tilapia and Corn Stew

Chesapeake Bay—Style Catfish

Pan-Fried Catfish with
Caper-Herb Sauce

Marseille-Style Bouillabaisse

Stir-Fried Shrimp and
Zucchini in Coconut Sauce

Curry-Dusted Shrimp
with Mango-Ginger Sauce

Shrimp with Bok Choy
and Baby Corn

Crispy Peppery Shrimp
in the Shell

Sweet and Tangy Scallops

Watercress, Scallop, and
Noodle Soup

Pasta with Red Clam Sauce

Capellini with Mussels
in Tomato-Basil Sauce

Salmon Cakes with Red Pepper Mayonnaise

SERVES 4

1 (14¾-ounce) can red salmon, drained, skin and large bones discarded

½ cup plain dried bread crumbs

3 scallions, chopped

¼ cup + 3 tablespoons fat-free mayonnaise

1 large egg, lightly beaten

2 tablespoons chopped fresh dill

¼ teaspoon black pepper

1 (5-ounce) jar roasted red pepper, well drained

⅛ teaspoon hot pepper sauce

2 tablespoons chopped gherkins or pickles

1 To make the salmon cakes, put the salmon in a medium bowl and flake with a fork. Add the bread crumbs, scallions, ¼ cup of the mayonnaise, the egg, dill, and black pepper; stir to combine well. With damp hands, shape the mixture into 4 (½-inch-thick) patties.

2 Spray a large nonstick skillet with nonstick spray and set over medium-high heat. Add the patties and cook until browned and heated through, 3–4 minutes on each side. Transfer to a platter.

3 Meanwhile, to make the red pepper mayonnaise, combine the roasted pepper, the remaining 3 tablespoons mayonnaise, and the pepper sauce in a blender; puree. Add the gherkins and pulse just until combined. Serve with the salmon cakes.

Per serving (1 salmon cake and 2 tablespoons red pepper mayonnaise): 210 Cal, 7 g Fat, 2 g Sat Fat, 0 g Trans Fat, 119 mg Chol, 801 mg Sod, 17 g Carb, 2 g Fib, 22 g Prot, 252 mg Calc. *PointsPlus* value: **5.**

◆ Filling Extra

Make a quick slaw to accompany this dish. Combine 3 cups coleslaw mix with 1 tablespoon lemon juice and salt and black pepper to taste.

*Salmon Cakes with
Red Pepper Mayonnaise*

Soy and Ginger—Marinated Salmon

SERVES 4

2 tablespoons unseasoned rice vinegar

1 tablespoon reduced-sodium soy sauce

1 tablespoon packed brown sugar

1 tablespoon grated peeled fresh ginger

1 garlic clove, minced

2 teaspoons Asian (dark) sesame oil

1 (1-pound) skinless salmon fillet, cut crosswise into 8 strips

4 cups lightly packed baby arugula

2 tablespoons chopped fresh chives

1 tablespoon black sesame seeds

1 To make the marinade, combine the vinegar, soy sauce, brown sugar, ginger, garlic, and 1 teaspoon of the sesame oil in a large bowl. Transfer 2 tablespoons of the mixture to a medium bowl and add the salmon, turning to coat; let marinate about 5 minutes.

2 Heat the remaining 1 teaspoon sesame oil in a large nonstick skillet over medium-high heat. Add the salmon and cook until just opaque in the center, about 2 minutes on each side.

3 Add the arugula to the remaining vinegar mixture and toss to coat. Divide the arugula evenly among 4 plates. Top each serving with 2 salmon strips and sprinkle with ½ tablespoon of the chives and ¾ teaspoon of the sesame seeds.

Per serving (1 cup salad and 2 salmon strips): 220 Cal, 10 g Fat, 2 g Sat Fat, 0 g Trans Fat, 74 mg Chol, 225 mg Sod, 7 g Carb, 1 g Fib, 26 g Prot, 104 mg Calc. *PointsPlus* value: **5.**

Orange and Lime—Marinated Halibut

SERVES 4

1 teaspoon grated orange zest

3 tablespoons orange juice

1 teaspoon grated lime zest

2 tablespoons lime juice

1 tablespoon reduced-sodium
soy sauce

½ teaspoon salt

¼ teaspoon black pepper

2 (¾-pound) halibut steaks

2 navel oranges, peeled and
sectioned, juice reserved

1 Spray the rack of a broiler pan with nonstick spray and preheat the broiler.

2 Combine the orange zest and juice, lime zest and juice, soy sauce, salt, and pepper in a baking dish large enough to hold the fish in a single layer. Add the halibut steaks and marinate about 5 minutes, turning once. Remove the halibut from the marinade; discard the marinade.

3 Place the halibut on the broiler rack and broil 4 inches from the heat until just opaque in the center, 3–4 minutes on each side.

4 Cut each halibut steak in half and place a portion on each of 4 plates. Top each piece of fish with one-fourth of the orange sections and drizzle evenly with the reserved orange juice.

Per serving (½ halibut steak and ½ orange): 217 Cal,
4 g Fat, 1 g Sat Fat, 0 g Trans Fat, 52 mg Chol,
302 mg Sod, 9 g Carb, 2 g Fib, 35 g Prot, 107 mg Calc.
PointsPlus value: **5.**

Swordfish with Asian Flavors

SERVES 4

3 tablespoons reduced-sodium soy sauce

3 tablespoons unseasoned rice vinegar

2 tablespoons packed brown sugar

1 teaspoon Asian (dark) sesame oil

2 teaspoons cornstarch

¼ teaspoon hot pepper sauce

4 (6-ounce) swordfish steaks, about ¾ inch thick

½ teaspoon salt

¼ teaspoon black pepper

2 teaspoons canola oil

1 tablespoon sesame seeds

1 Stir together the soy sauce, vinegar, brown sugar, sesame oil, cornstarch, and pepper sauce in a small bowl until smooth; set aside.

2 Sprinkle the swordfish with the salt and pepper.

3 Heat the oil in a large nonstick skillet over medium-high heat. Add the swordfish and cook until just opaque throughout, about 4 minutes on each side; transfer to a platter. Stir the cornstarch mixture and add to the skillet. Cook, stirring constantly, until the sauce thickens and bubbles, about 1 minute. Spoon over the swordfish and sprinkle with the sesame seeds.

Per serving (1 swordfish steak and generous 1 tablespoon sauce): 228 Cal, 11 g Fat, 2 g Sat Fat, 0 g Trans Fat, 66 mg Chol, 765 mg Sod, 9 g Carb, 0 g Fib, 23 g Prot, 23 mg Calc. **PointsPlus** value: **7.**

Mediterranean-Style Swordfish

SERVES 4

1 tablespoon chopped fresh
   parsley

Grated zest of ½ lemon

1 tablespoon lemon juice

2 teaspoons Dijon mustard

1½ teaspoons olive oil

¾ teaspoon dried basil

½ teaspoon salt

¼ teaspoon black pepper

4 (6-ounce) swordfish steaks,
   about ¾ inch thick

2 tablespoons chopped pitted
   kalamata olives

1 Combine the parsley, lemon zest and juice, mustard, oil, basil, ¼ teaspoon of the salt, and ⅛ teaspoon of the pepper in a small bowl; set aside.

2 Sprinkle the swordfish with the remaining ¼ teaspoon salt and ⅛ teaspoon pepper. Spray a nonstick ridged grill pan with nonstick spray and set over medium-high heat. Place the swordfish on the grill pan and cook until browned, about 4 minutes on each side. Brush with half of the parsley mixture; turn and grill about 1 minute. Brush with the remaining parsley mixture; turn and grill until the fish is just opaque throughout, about 1 minute longer. Serve sprinkled with the olives.

Per serving (1 garnished swordfish steak): 198 Cal, 9 g Fat, 2 g Sat Fat, 0 g Trans Fat, 80 mg Chol, 495 mg Sod, 1 g Carb, 0 g Fib, 26 g Prot, 23 mg Calc. *PointsPlus* value: **5.**

◈ Filling Extra

For a tasty good-for-you side dish, toss cooked bulgur with finely chopped red bell pepper and grated lemon zest (½ cup cooked bulgur per serving will increase the *PointsPlus* value by **2**).

Sesame-Crusted Tuna Steaks

SERVES 4

3 tablespoons apple-cider vinegar

2 tablespoons honey

1 tablespoon Asian (dark) sesame oil

2 tablespoons chopped red bell pepper

1 tablespoon chopped fresh chives

¾ teaspoon salt

¼ teaspoon black pepper

4 (6-ounce) tuna steaks, ½ inch thick

2 tablespoons sesame seeds

1 To prepare the topping, combine the vinegar, honey, sesame oil, bell pepper, chives, ¼ teaspoon of the salt, and ⅛ teaspoon of the black pepper in a serving dish; set aside.

2 Sprinkle the tuna steaks with the remaining ½ teaspoon salt and ⅛ teaspoon black pepper. Spread the sesame seeds on a plate; coat the tuna with the seeds, pressing lightly so they adhere.

3 Spray a large nonstick skillet with nonstick spray and set over medium-high heat. Add the tuna and cook 3–4 minutes on each side for medium-rare or until desired doneness. Serve with the bell pepper topping.

Per serving (1 tuna steak and about 2 tablespoons topping): 263 Cal, 7 g Fat, 1 g Sat Fat, 0 g Trans Fat, 74 mg Chol, 499 mg Sod, 10 g Carb, 1 g Fib, 39 g Prot, 34 mg Calc. *PointsPlus* value: **6.**

Sesame-Crusted Tuna Steaks

Bayou-Style Tuna with Roasted Pepper Sauce

SERVES 4

1 tablespoon smoked sweet paprika

1½ teaspoons sugar

½ teaspoon ground cumin

½ teaspoon dried oregano

1 teaspoon salt

½ teaspoon black pepper

4 (6-ounce) tuna steaks, ½ inch thick

1 tablespoon olive oil

1 (5-ounce) jar roasted red pepper, rinsed and drained

⅓ cup fat-free half-and-half

1 garlic clove, peeled

1 Combine the paprika, sugar, cumin, oregano, ¾ teaspoon of the salt, and the black pepper on a sheet of wax paper. Coat the tuna steaks with the paprika mixture, pressing lightly so it adheres.

2 Heat the oil in a large nonstick skillet over high heat. Add the tuna and cook about 3 minutes on each side for medium-rare or until desired doneness.

3 Meanwhile, combine the roasted pepper, half-and-half, garlic, and the remaining ¼ teaspoon salt in a blender and puree. Transfer to a microwavable bowl and microwave on High, stirring twice, until bubbly, 1–1½ minutes.

4 Spoon the sauce evenly on 4 plates and top each with a tuna steak.

Per serving (1 tuna steak and 3 tablespoons sauce): 224 Cal, 6 g Fat, 1 g Sat Fat, 0 g Trans Fat, 95 mg Chol, 820 mg Sod, 7 g Carb, 1 g Fib, 34 g Prot, 56 mg Calc. *PointsPlus* value: **6**.

Greek-Style Cod Fillets

SERVES 4

2 teaspoons olive oil

1 onion, chopped

2 garlic cloves, minced

2 (14½-ounce) cans diced tomatoes

½ teaspoon dried oregano

¼ teaspoon black pepper

4 (5-ounce) cod fillets

¼ teaspoon salt

4 tablespoons crumbled fat-free feta cheese

1 Heat the oil in a large nonstick skillet over medium heat. Add the onion and garlic; cook, stirring, until softened, about 4 minutes. Add the tomatoes with their juice, the oregano, and pepper; cook, stirring, until heated through, about 3 minutes.

2 Sprinkle the cod with the salt. Place in the skillet and spoon some of the tomato mixture on top. Cook, covered, until the fish is just opaque in the center, 6–8 minutes. Sprinkle with the feta.

Per serving (1 cod fillet, ¾ cup sauce, and 1 tablespoon feta): 217 Cal, 4 g Fat, 1 g Sat Fat, 0 g Trans Fat, 76 mg Chol, 559 mg Sod, 12 g Carb, 3 g Fib, 33 g Prot, 96 mg Calc. *PointsPlus* value: **4.**

⏱ Time-Saver

Instead of crumbling the cheese by hand, use packaged crumbled feta cheese, found in the gourmet cheese section of the supermarket.

Microwave Creole Cod

SERVES 4

1 green bell pepper, chopped

1 red bell pepper, chopped

2 celery stalks, chopped

1 onion, chopped

2 garlic cloves, minced

1½ teaspoons Creole or Cajun
seasoning

1 (8-ounce) can tomato sauce

1 large tomato, chopped

1¼ pounds cod fillet, cut into
4 equal pieces

1 Combine the bell peppers, celery, onion, garlic, and Creole seasoning in a large microwavable bowl. Cover and microwave on High, stirring once, until tender, about 5 minutes. Pour off any liquid.

2 Stir in the tomato sauce and tomato. Microwave, uncovered, on High until heated through, about 3 minutes. Set aside.

3 Spray a microwavable shallow baking dish with nonstick spray. Place the cod in the dish in a single layer; cover and microwave on High, until just opaque in the center, about 4 minutes. Serve with the sauce.

Per serving (1 piece cod and about 1 cup sauce): 181 Cal, 2 g Fat, 0 g Sat Fat, 0 g Trans Fat, 75 mg Chol, 637 mg Sod, 12 g Carb, 3 g Fib, 29 g Prot, 54 mg Calc. **PointsPlus** value: **4.**

⏱ Time-Saver

The sauce can be prepared the day before. Prepare as directed through step 2, then let cool. Cover and refrigerate overnight. To reheat, microwave, uncovered, on High until heated through, 1–2 minutes.

Mahimahi with Shallot-Mustard Sauce

SERVES 4

4 (¼-pound) mahimahi fillets

½ teaspoon dried thyme

½ teaspoon salt

¼ + ⅛ teaspoon black pepper

2 teaspoons olive oil

2 shallots, finely chopped

¼ cup dry white wine

½ cup bottled clam juice

2 tablespoons coarse-grained
   Dijon mustard

1 Sprinkle the mahimahi fillets with the thyme, salt, and ¼ teaspoon of the pepper. Heat the oil in a large nonstick skillet over medium-high heat. Add the mahimahi and cook until just opaque in the center, about 3 minutes on each side. Transfer to a plate and keep warm.

2 Add the shallots to the skillet and cook, stirring, until softened, about 5 minutes. Add the wine and cook, stirring, until reduced by half, about 3 minutes. Whisk in the clam juice, mustard, and the remaining ⅛ teaspoon pepper; bring to a simmer and cook about 1 minute. Serve with the mahimahi.

Per serving (1 mahimahi fillet and generous 2 tablespoons sauce): 149 Cal, 4 g Fat, 1 g Sat Fat, 0 g Trans Fat, 63 mg Chol, 645 mg Sod, 3 g Carb, 0 g Fib, 23 g Prot, 34 mg Calc. **PointsPlus** value: **4.**

Snapper with Easy Pesto Sauce

SERVES 4

4 (¼-pound) skinless red snapper fillets

1 zucchini, cut on the diagonal into ¼-inch slices

1 yellow bell pepper, cut lengthwise into 8 pieces

½ teaspoon salt

¼ teaspoon black pepper

1 small head radicchio, cut into 8 wedges

3 tablespoons prepared pesto

1 tablespoon balsamic vinegar

1 Spray the rack of a broiler pan with nonstick spray and preheat the broiler.

2 Lightly spray the snapper, zucchini, and bell pepper with nonstick spray; sprinkle with the salt and black pepper. Arrange on the broiler rack in a single layer and broil 4 inches from the heat until lightly browned, about 4 minutes. Turn the snapper, zucchini, and bell pepper; add the radicchio to the broiler rack. Broil until the snapper is just opaque in the center, the zucchini and bell pepper are tender, and the radicchio is slightly wilted, about 4 minutes.

3 Meanwhile, combine the pesto and vinegar in a cup. Arrange the fish and vegetables on a platter. Drizzle with the pesto sauce.

Per serving (1 snapper fillet, ¼ of vegetables, and 1 tablespoon sauce): 208 Cal, 8 g Fat, 2 g Sat Fat, 0 g Trans Fat, 77 mg Chol, 520 mg Sod, 4 g Carb, 1 g Fib, 29 g Prot, 80 mg Calc. *PointsPlus* value: **5.**

Striped Bass with Cherry Tomato—Caper Sauce

SERVES 4

1 teaspoon ground cumin

½ teaspoon salt

¼ teaspoon black pepper

4 (6-ounce) striped bass fillets

2 teaspoons olive oil

2 cups red cherry tomatoes, halved

2 cups yellow cherry tomatoes, halved

1 red onion, chopped

2 tablespoons capers, drained

1 tablespoon lemon juice

1 scallion, thinly sliced

2⅔ cups hot cooked whole-wheat couscous

1 Combine the cumin, ¼ teaspoon of the salt, and ⅛ teaspoon of the pepper in a small bowl; sprinkle over the striped bass. Heat the oil in a large nonstick skillet over medium-high heat. Add the fillets, skin side up, and cook until just opaque in the center, about 4 minutes on each side. Transfer to a platter and keep warm.

2 Add the tomatoes and onion to the skillet; cook, stirring, about 3 minutes. Add the capers, lemon juice, and the remaining ¼ teaspoon salt and ⅛ teaspoon pepper; cook about 1 minute longer. Spoon the tomato mixture over the bass. Sprinkle the scallion over the couscous and serve alongside.

Per serving (1 bass fillet, ⅔ cup sauce, and ⅔ cup couscous): 391 Cal, 10 g Fat, 2 g Sat Fat, 0 g Trans Fat, 80 mg Chol, 538 mg Sod, 38 g Carb, 7 g Fib, 39 g Prot, 99 mg Calc. **PointsPlus** value: **8.**

Sea Bass with Green Sauce

SERVES 4

4 (6-ounce) sea bass fillets

¾ teaspoon salt

¼ teaspoon black pepper

¼ cup lightly packed fresh parsley

¼ cup chopped scallions

¼ cup lightly packed tender watercress sprigs

2 quarter-size slices peeled fresh ginger

3 tablespoons white-wine vinegar

2 tablespoons water

2 tablespoons olive oil

1 Sprinkle the sea bass with ½ teaspoon of the salt and the pepper. Spray a large nonstick skillet with olive oil nonstick spray and set over medium-high heat. Add the fillets, skin side up, and cook until just opaque in the center, about 4 minutes on each side. Transfer to a platter and keep warm.

2 Combine the parsley, scallions, watercress, ginger, vinegar, water, oil, and the remaining ¼ teaspoon salt in a food processor or blender and puree. Spoon the sauce over the fish.

Per serving (1 bass fillet and about 2 tablespoons sauce): 229 Cal, 10 g Fat, 2 g Sat Fat, 0 g Trans Fat, 68 mg Chol, 571 mg Sod, 2 g Carb, 1 g Fib, 31 g Prot, 41 mg Calc. **PointsPlus** value: **6.**

Filling Extra

A large baked sweet potato is a great way to get a dose of fiber and beta carotene (vitamin A). One large baked sweet potato per serving will increase the **PointsPlus** value by **4.**

Parmesan and Potato—Crusted Flounder with Tomato-Cilantro Sauce

SERVES 4

3 tomatoes, chopped

½ small onion, chopped

3 tablespoons chopped fresh cilantro

1½ tablespoons red-wine vinegar

¼ teaspoon salt

1 large egg

⅔ cup instant mashed potato flakes

2 tablespoons grated Parmesan cheese

½ teaspoon black pepper

4 (¼-pound) flounder fillets

1 tablespoon olive oil

1 To make the sauce, combine the tomatoes, onion, cilantro, vinegar, and salt in a serving bowl; set aside.

2 Lightly beat the egg in a large shallow bowl or pie plate. Combine the potato flakes, Parmesan, and pepper on a sheet of wax paper. Dip each fillet into the egg to coat on both sides, then into the potato mixture, pressing lightly so it adheres.

3 Heat the oil in a large nonstick skillet over medium-high heat. Add the flounder, in batches if necessary, and cook until browned and just opaque in the center, 2–3 minutes on each side. Serve with the sauce.

Per serving (1 flounder fillet and generous ¼ cup sauce): 205 Cal, 7 g Fat, 2 g Sat Fat, 0 g Trans Fat, 111 mg Chol, 322 mg Sod, 11 g Carb, 2 g Fib, 24 g Prot, 72 mg Calc. **PointsPlus** value: **5.**

⏱ Time-Saver

Skip step 1 and substitute 1 cup of your favorite prepared mild salsa.

Ham-Wrapped Flounder with Spinach Stuffing

SERVES 4

4 (¼-pound) flounder fillets

¼ teaspoon black pepper

1 cup lightly packed baby spinach

4 thin slices baked ham

2 teaspoons butter

2 teaspoons olive oil

2 tablespoons dry vermouth or reduced-sodium chicken broth

1 tablespoon lemon juice

Chopped fresh parsley

4 lemon wedges

1 Sprinkle the flounder fillets with the pepper and top evenly with the spinach. Roll up the fillets, then wrap each one in a slice of ham.

2 Melt the butter with the oil in a large nonstick skillet over medium heat. Add the flounder rolls and cook, turning occasionally, until the fish is just opaque in the center and the ham is lightly browned, about 8 minutes. Transfer the flounder rolls to a platter and keep warm.

3 Add the vermouth and lemon juice to the skillet; cook, scraping up any browned bits from the bottom of the pan, about 30 seconds. Drizzle the sauce over the flounder and sprinkle with the parsley. Serve with the lemon wedges.

Per serving (1 flounder roll and about ½ tablespoon sauce): 156 Cal, 6 g Fat, 2 g Sat Fat, 0 g Trans Fat, 65 mg Chol, 278 mg Sod, 1 g Carb, 0 g Fib, 22 g Prot, 27 mg Calc. *PointsPlus* value: **4.**

*Ham-Wrapped Flounder
with Spinach Stuffing*

Orange Roughy with Spicy Tomato Sauce

SERVES 4

4 (6-ounce) skinless boneless orange roughy or tilapia fillets

¾ teaspoon salt

¼ teaspoon black pepper

4 teaspoons extra-virgin olive oil

3 garlic cloves, minced

1 (14½-ounce) can diced tomatoes with green pepper and onion

2 tablespoons chopped fresh parsley

1 tablespoon capers, drained

½ teaspoon dried oregano

¼ teaspoon crushed red pepper

1 Sprinkle the orange roughy fillets with ½ teaspoon of the salt and ⅛ teaspoon of the black pepper. Heat 2 teaspoons of the oil in a large nonstick skillet over medium-high heat. Add the fillets and cook until just opaque in the center, 2–3 minutes on each side. Transfer to a platter and keep warm.

2 Add the remaining 2 teaspoons oil to the skillet. Add the garlic and cook, stirring, until fragrant, about 30 seconds. Add the tomatoes with their juice, the parsley, capers, oregano, crushed red pepper, and the remaining ¼ teaspoon salt and ⅛ teaspoon black pepper. Cook until the mixture starts to thicken, 3–4 minutes. Return the fish to the skillet and cook just until heated through, about 1 minute longer.

Per serving (1 orange roughly fillet and ¼ cup sauce): 236 Cal, 7 g Fat, 1 g Sat Fat, 0 g Trans Fat, 94 mg Chol, 946 mg Sod, 8 g Carb, 1 g Fib, 34 g Prot, 64 mg Calc. **PointsPlus** value: **5.**

◆ Filling Extra

Round out this flavorful main dish with brown rice (½ cup cooked brown rice per serving will increase the **PointsPlus** value by **3**).

Tilapia and Corn Stew

SERVES 4

2 teaspoons olive oil

2 garlic cloves, minced

1 yellow bell pepper, chopped

1 red bell pepper, chopped

1 (14½-ounce) can diced
  tomatoes with green chiles

1 (10-ounce) package frozen corn
  kernels

1 cup frozen baby lima beans

¼ teaspoon dried oregano

¼ teaspoon salt

1 pound tilapia or skinless
  halibut fillets, cut into 1-inch
  pieces

2 scallions, chopped

2 tablespoons chopped fresh
  parsley

1 Heat the oil in a nonstick Dutch oven over medium-high heat. Add the garlic and cook, stirring, until light golden, about 1 minute. Add the bell peppers and cook, stirring, until softened, about 2 minutes.

2 Add the tomatoes with their juice, the corn, lima beans, oregano, and salt; bring to a boil. Add the tilapia, stirring gently to coat the fillets with the liquid; return to a boil. Reduce the heat and simmer, covered, until the tilapia is just opaque in the center, about 6 minutes. Ladle the stew into 4 bowls; sprinkle each serving evenly with the scallions and parsley.

Per serving (about 1 ⅔ cups): 261 Cal, 5 g Fat, 1 g Sat Fat, 0 g Trans Fat, 60 mg Chol, 430 mg Sod, 30 g Carb, 6 g Fib, 27 g Prot, 80 mg Calc. **PointsPlus** value: **7.**

Chesapeake Bay—Style Catfish

SERVES 4

⅓ cup fat-free mayonnaise

1½ tablespoons lemon juice

¼ teaspoon garlic powder

¼ teaspoon onion powder

¼ teaspoon celery seeds

4 (¼-pound) catfish fillets

¾ teaspoon salt

¼ teaspoon black pepper

⅛ teaspoon cayenne

2 teaspoons canola oil

1 Combine the mayonnaise, lemon juice, garlic powder, onion powder, and celery seeds in a small bowl; set aside.

2 Sprinkle the catfish fillets with the salt, pepper, and cayenne. Heat the oil in a large nonstick skillet over medium-high heat. Add the fillets and cook until just opaque in the center, about 3 minutes on each side.

3 Place 1 fillet on each of 4 plates and top each serving with a dollop of the lemon mayonnaise.

Per serving (1 catfish fillet and 1½ tablespoons lemon mayonnaise): 204 Cal, 10 g Fat, 2 g Sat Fat, 0 g Trans Fat, 88 mg Chol, 666 mg Sod, 3 g Carb, 1 g Fib, 23 g Prot, 59 mg Calc. *PointsPlus* value: **5.**

Pan-Fried Catfish with Caper-Herb Sauce

SERVES 4

1 cup lightly packed flat-leaf parsley leaves

¼ cup lightly packed fresh cilantro leaves

2 tablespoons capers, drained

2 tablespoons red-wine vinegar

2 tablespoons water

2 teaspoons canola oil

4 (¼-pound) catfish fillets

2 teaspoons Old Bay seasoning

⅛ teaspoon black pepper

2 large tomatoes, preferably heirloom, each cut into 8 slices

1 Combine the parsley, cilantro, capers, vinegar, water, and 1 teaspoon of the oil in a blender or food processor and puree; set aside.

2 Sprinkle the catfish fillets with the Old Bay seasoning and pepper. Heat the remaining 1 teaspoon oil in a large nonstick skillet over medium-high heat. Add the fillets and cook until just opaque in the center, about 3 minutes on each side.

3 Arrange 4 tomato slices in an overlapping row on each of 4 plates; top each serving with a fillet and drizzle evenly with the sauce.

Per serving (4 tomato slices, 1 catfish fillet, and about 2 tablespoons sauce): 213 Cal, 10 g Fat, 2 g Sat Fat, 0 g Trans Fat, 86 g Chol, 527 mg Sod, 6 g Carb, 2 g Fib, 25 g Prot, 93 mg Calc. **PointsPlus** value: **5.**

⏱ Time-Saver

Instead of slicing the large tomatoes, garnish each serving with ½ cup grape tomatoes.

Stir-Fried Shrimp and Zucchini in Coconut Sauce

SERVES 4

2 teaspoons canola oil

1 pound peeled and deveined large shrimp

3 medium zucchini, cut into 2 x ¼-inch matchsticks

2 red bell peppers, cut into thin strips

3 scallions, sliced

1 tablespoon grated peeled fresh ginger

2 garlic cloves, minced

1 teaspoon Thai red curry paste

½ cup light coconut milk

1½ tablespoons Asian fish sauce

1 tablespoon packed brown sugar

1 Heat 1 teaspoon of the oil in a nonstick wok or large deep nonstick skillet over medium-high heat. When a drop of water sizzles in it, add the shrimp and stir-fry until just opaque in the center, about 3 minutes. Transfer to a large bowl.

2 Heat the remaining 1 teaspoon oil in the wok. Add the zucchini, bell peppers, and scallions; stir-fry until crisp-tender, about 2 minutes. Add the ginger, garlic, and curry paste; stir-fry until fragrant, about 30 seconds. Add to the bowl.

3 Add the coconut milk, fish sauce, and brown sugar to the wok; bring to a simmer. Cook, stirring frequently, about 3 minutes. Return the shrimp and vegetables to the wok; stir-fry until heated through, about 1 minute longer.

Per serving (about 1½ cups): 186 Cal, 5 g Fat, 1 g Sat Fat, 0 g Trans Fat, 161 mg Chol, 735 mg Sod, 16 g Carb, 3 g Fib, 21 g Prot, 78 mg Calc. *PointsPlus* value: **5.**

Time-Saver

If you're in a rush, substitute ⅛ teaspoon ground ginger for the fresh ginger.

Curry-Dusted Shrimp with Mango-Ginger Sauce

SERVES 4

1 tablespoon Madras curry powder

¾ teaspoon salt

1 pound peeled and deveined extra-large shrimp

2 mangoes, peeled, pitted, and cut into chunks (about 2 cups)

¼ cup water

1½ teaspoons honey

2 teaspoons canola oil

1 small onion, finely chopped

1 tablespoon minced peeled fresh ginger

Pinch cayenne

2 tablespoons chopped fresh cilantro

1 Combine the curry powder and ½ teaspoon of the salt in a medium bowl. Add the shrimp and toss to coat evenly; set aside.

2 Combine the mangoes, water, and honey in a blender or food processor and puree; set aside.

3 Heat the oil in a medium nonstick saucepan over medium-high heat. Add the onion, ginger, cayenne, and the remaining ¼ teaspoon salt; cook, stirring frequently, until lightly browned, about 3 minutes. Add the mango puree and bring to a boil, stirring occasionally. Reduce the heat and simmer about 1 minute. Pour the sauce into a sauceboat.

4 Spray a large nonstick skillet with nonstick spray and set over medium-high heat. Add the shrimp and cook until just opaque in the center, about 2 minutes on each side. Transfer to a platter and sprinkle with the cilantro. Serve with the sauce.

Per serving (about 7 shrimp and ⅓ cup sauce): 194 Cal, 4 g Fat, 1 g Sat Fat, 0 g Trans Fat, 161 mg Chol, 633 mg Sod, 23 g Carb, 3 g Fib, 18 g Prot, 56 mg Calc. *PointsPlus* value: **5.**

⏱ Time-Saver

Use refrigerated sliced peeled fresh mangoes. They're available in jars in the produce section of some supermarkets.

Shrimp with Bok Choy and Baby Corn

SERVES 4

2 tablespoons hoisin sauce

2 tablespoons reduced-sodium soy sauce

2 tablespoons dry vermouth or dry sherry

2 teaspoons cornstarch

3 teaspoons Asian (dark) sesame oil

1¼ pounds peeled and deveined large shrimp

1 tablespoon grated peeled fresh ginger

2 garlic cloves, minced

1 pound bok choy, cut crosswise into 2-inch pieces

1 small red onion, thinly sliced

1 (8-ounce) can baby corn, drained

2 teaspoons sesame seeds

2 cups hot cooked quick-cooking brown rice

1 Stir together the hoisin sauce, soy sauce, vermouth, and cornstarch in a small bowl until smooth; set aside.

2 Heat 2 teaspoons of the sesame oil in a nonstick wok or large deep nonstick skillet over medium-high heat. Add the shrimp and stir-fry until just opaque in the center, 3–4 minutes. Transfer to a medium bowl; set aside.

3 Add the remaining 1 teaspoon sesame oil, the ginger, and garlic to the wok; stir-fry about 30 seconds. Add the bok choy and onion; stir-fry until crisp-tender, about 3 minutes. Add the baby corn, shrimp, and hoisin mixture; stir-fry until the sauce thickens and bubbles about 1 minute longer. Sprinkle with the sesame seeds. Serve with the rice.

Per serving (1½ cups shrimp mixture and ½ cup rice): 316 Cal, 7 g Fat, 1 g Sat Fat, 0 g Trans Fat, 202 mg Chol, 736 mg Sod, 36 g Carb, 5 g Fib, 27 g Prot, 125 mg Calc. *PointsPlus* value: **8.**

Shrimp with Bok Choy and Baby Corn

Crispy Peppery Shrimp in the Shell

SERVES 4

1½ pounds extra-large shrimp, unpeeled

1 tablespoon extra-virgin olive oil

1 tablespoon kosher salt

½ teaspoon black pepper

1 Place an oven rack in the upper third of the oven and preheat the oven to 450°F. Spray a heavy baking sheet with olive oil nonstick spray.

2 With a small sharp knife or small kitchen scissors, cut along the back of each shrimp through the shell just deep enough to expose the vein; remove the vein, leaving the shell intact.

3 Toss together the shrimp, oil, salt, and pepper in a large bowl until coated evenly. Arrange the shrimp in a single layer on the baking sheet. Roast in the oven, without turning, until just opaque in the center, about 5 minutes.

Per serving (about 7 shrimp): 96 Cal, 3 g Fat, 0 g Sat Fat, 0 g Trans Fat, 160 mg Chol, 767 mg Sod, 0 g Carb, 0 g Fib, 17 g Prot, 33 mg Calc. **PointsPlus** value: **3.**

Filling Extra

If you like, steam 2 cups each broccoli and cauliflower florets to serve alongside the shrimp.

Sweet and Tangy Scallops

SERVES 4

2 teaspoons olive oil

1 onion, chopped

2 garlic cloves, minced

½ teaspoon ground ginger

Pinch crushed red pepper

1 red bell pepper, chopped

1 cup reduced-sodium vegetable broth

¼ cup dark raisins

1 tablespoon lime juice

½ teaspoon salt

1 pound sea scallops (about 24)

¼ cup chopped fresh cilantro

1 Heat the oil in a large nonstick skillet over medium-high heat. Add the onion, garlic, ginger, and crushed red pepper. Cook, stirring until the onion is softened, about 3 minutes. Add the bell pepper and cook, stirring occasionally, until crisp-tender, about 2 minutes. Add the broth, raisins, lime juice, and salt; bring to a boil. Reduce the heat and simmer about 5 minutes.

2 Add the scallops to the skillet and simmer, covered, until just opaque in the center, about 5 minutes. Stir in the cilantro.

Per serving (about 6 scallops and ½ cup broth with vegetables): 136 Cal, 3 g Fat, 0 g Sat Fat, 0 g Trans Fat, 32 mg Chol, 580 mg Sod, 13 g Carb, 1 g Fib, 14 g Prot, 98 mg Calc. **PointsPlus** value: **5.**

Watercress, Scallop, and Noodle Soup

SERVES 4

2 teaspoons Asian (dark) sesame oil

1 tablespoon minced peeled fresh ginger

2 garlic cloves, minced

5 cups bottled clam juice

2 tablespoons white miso

6 ounces thin spaghetti, broken into 3-inch lengths

1 pound sea scallops

1 (5-ounce) bag watercress

2 scallions, sliced

1 Heat the sesame oil in a nonstick Dutch oven over medium heat. Add the ginger and garlic; cook, stirring constantly, until fragrant, about 30 seconds. Add the clam juice, miso, and spaghetti; bring to a boil over medium-high heat. Reduce the heat and simmer, stirring occasionally, about 3 minutes.

2 Add the scallops and watercress to the Dutch oven; simmer until the scallops are just opaque in the center and the noodles are tender, about 4 minutes longer. Ladle the soup into 4 bowls and sprinkle evenly with the scallions.

Per serving (about 6 scallops and 1¼ cups broth with noodles): 293 Cal, 5 g Fat, 1 g Sat Fat, 0 g Trans Fat, 39 mg Chol, 1146 mg Sod, 40 g Carb, 5 g Fib, 23 g Prot, 172 mg Calc. *PointsPlus* value: **7.**

⏱ Time-Saver

Use fine egg noodles instead of breaking the spaghetti into pieces.

Pasta with Red Clam Sauce

SERVES 4

1 (9-ounce) package fresh
   linguine or fettuccine

2 teaspoons olive oil

3 garlic cloves, minced

2 (6½-ounce) cans chopped
   clams, drained, liquid from
   1 can reserved

1 (14-ounce) can diced tomatoes

½ teaspoon dried oregano

¼ teaspoon crushed red pepper

1 Cook the linguine according to the package directions, omitting the salt if desired; drain.

2 Meanwhile, heat the oil in a large nonstick skillet over medium-high heat. Add the garlic and cook, stirring, until golden, about 2 minutes. Add the clams and reserved liquid, the tomatoes with their juice, the oregano, and crushed red pepper; bring to a boil. Cook, stirring occasionally, until the sauce thickens, about 7 minutes. Add the linguine and toss to coat.

Per serving (about 1¼ cups): 330 Cal, 5 g Fat, 1 g Sat Fat, 0 g Trans Fat, 28 mg Chol, 426 mg Sod, 51 g Carb, 4 g Fib, 20 g Prot, 87 mg Calc. *PointsPlus* value: **8.**

Capellini with Mussels in Tomato-Basil Sauce

SERVES 4

6 ounces capellini

1 tablespoon extra-virgin olive oil

1 onion, chopped

3 large garlic cloves, minced

1 (14½-ounce) can diced tomatoes

½ cup dry white wine

2 pounds mussels, scrubbed

¼ cup chopped fresh basil

1 Cook the capellini according to the package directions, omitting the salt if desired. Drain, reserving ½ cup of the cooking water.

2 Meanwhile, heat the oil in a nonstick Dutch oven over medium-high heat. Add the onion and garlic; cook, stirring, until softened, about 5 minutes. Add the tomatoes with their juice and the wine; bring to a boil. Reduce the heat and simmer about 2 minutes.

3 Add the mussels to the Dutch oven. Cook, covered, until they open, about 5 minutes. Discard any mussels that do not open. Stir in the basil and the reserved cooking water. Transfer the capellini to a platter and top with the mussels and sauce.

Per serving (2 cups mussels in shells and ¾ cup pasta with sauce): 304 Cal, 5 g Fat, 1 g Sat Fat, 0 g Trans Fat, 22 mg Chol, 536 mg Sod, 47 g Carb, 4 g Fib, 17 g Prot, 88 mg Calc. **PointsPlus** value: **8.**

◆ Filling Extra

Start your meal with a crisp greens salad dressed with balsamic vinegar, salt, and pepper.

Capellini with Mussels in Tomato-Basil Sauce

Couscous and Vegetable–Stuffed Tomatoes

6

Meatless Ways for Great Suppers

Cavatelli with Escarole and
White Beans

Curried Vegetables with Lentils
and Couscous

Easy Red Beans and Rice

Herbed Bean and Tomato
Pita Pizzas

Cuban-Style Black Beans and Rice

Mediterranean-Style Salad Pizzas

Bread Salad with Tomatoes,
Beans, and Feta

Tomato, Avocado, and
Black Bean Tacos

Warm Lentil Salad with
Tahini Dressing

White Bean Bruschetta with Chopped
Salad

Spinach Fettuccine with
Tomato-Soy Ragu

Linguine with Creamy
Roasted Pepper Sauce

Gnocchi with Herb-Walnut Pesto

Double Cheese and Macaroni

Orzo with Spring Vegetables
and Ricotta

Vegetable-Topped Orange Couscous

Couscous and Vegetable—Stuffed
Tomatoes

Double Cheese Polenta with
Golden Onions

Tofu and Vegetable Lo Mein

Asian Vegetables in Coconut Curry

Mixed Vegetable and Tofu Stir-Fry

Brown Rice and Soy Burritos

Hunan-Style Vegetables and Tempeh

Tempeh and Black Bean Tostadas

Cabbage and Mushroom Fajitas

Portobello Mushroom—Garlic Burgers

Spanish Potato Tortilla

Microwave Vegetable Strata

Ricotta and Cheddar Cheese Omelette

Scrambled Eggs with Zucchini
and Scallions

Cavatelli with Escarole and White Beans

SERVES 4

8 ounces frozen cavatelli

1½ teaspoons extra-virgin olive oil

3 garlic cloves, minced

⅛ teaspoon crushed red pepper

1 pound escarole, trimmed and cut into 2-inch pieces

1 (15½-ounce) can small white beans, rinsed and drained

1 cup reduced-sodium chicken broth

¼ teaspoon salt

¼ cup grated Parmesan cheese

1 Cook the cavatelli according to the package directions, omitting the salt if desired; drain and keep warm.

2 Meanwhile, heat the oil in a Dutch oven over medium-high heat. Add the garlic and crushed red pepper; cook, stirring constantly, until fragrant, about 30 seconds. Add the escarole, a handful at a time, stirring until it has been incorporated. Add the beans and cook, stirring, until the escarole is wilted, about 2 minutes longer. Add the broth and salt; bring to a simmer. Cook until the broth is slightly reduced, about 4 minutes. Add the pasta and cook until heated through, about 1 minute longer. Remove the Dutch oven from the heat and stir in the Parmesan.

Per serving (1 cup): 359 Cal, 6 g Fat, 2 g Sat Fat, 0 g Trans Fat, 7 mg Chol, 779 mg Sod, 60 g Carb, 11 g Fib, 16 g Prot, 189 mg Calc. *PointsPlus* value: **10.**

⏱ Time-Saver

Substitute a 1-pound package of cut-up kale for the escarole and save yourself the prep. You'll find the kale by the bagged salads in the produce section of most supermarkets.

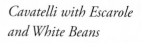
Cavatelli with Escarole and White Beans

Curried Vegetables with Lentils and Couscous

SERVES 4

¾ cup whole-wheat couscous

1 tablespoon canola oil

1 onion, thinly sliced

1 carrot, chopped

1 tablespoon grated peeled fresh ginger

2 teaspoons Madras curry powder

1 tomato, chopped

1 (15½-ounce) can lentils, rinsed and drained

½ cup golden raisins

¼ cup water

¼ teaspoon salt

1 Prepare the couscous according to the package directions, omitting the salt if desired. Set aside.

2 Meanwhile, heat the oil in a large nonstick skillet over high heat. Add the onion, carrot, ginger, and curry powder; cook, stirring, until the vegetables are softened, about 5 minutes. Add the tomato and cook about 2 minutes. Stir in the lentils, raisins, water, and salt; cook until the water is absorbed, about 3 minutes. Transfer the couscous to a serving bowl and top with the lentil mixture.

Per serving (½ cup couscous and about ⅔ cup lentil mixture): 308 Cal, 5 g Fat, 0 g Sat Fat, 0 g Trans Fat, 0 mg Chol, 645 mg Sod, 59 g Carb, 9 g Fib, 13 g Prot, 59 mg Calc. *PointsPlus* value: **7.**

◆ Filling Extra

Use 2 carrots instead of 1, and add a 5-ounce bag of baby spinach after the water is absorbed in step 2, stirring until the spinach wilts.

Easy Red Beans and Rice

SERVES 4

¾ cup quick-cooking brown rice

1 tablespoon olive oil

1 onion, chopped

4 scallions, thinly sliced

1 green bell pepper, finely
chopped

1 red bell pepper, finely
chopped

3 garlic cloves, minced

½ teaspoon salt

¼ teaspoon dried basil

¼ teaspoon black pepper

⅛ teaspoon cayenne

1 cup water

1 (15½-ounce) can red kidney
beans, rinsed and drained

1 Prepare the rice according to the package directions, omitting the fat; keep warm.

2 Heat the oil in a large nonstick skillet over medium-high heat. Add the onion, scallions, bell peppers, garlic, salt, basil, black pepper, and cayenne; cook, stirring frequently, until the vegetables begin to soften, about 5 minutes. Add the water and beans; bring to a boil. Reduce the heat and simmer until the mixture is slightly thickened, about 5 minutes. Serve over the rice.

Per serving (generous 1 cup bean mixture and scant ½ cup rice): 218 Cal, 4 g Fat, 1 g Sat Fat, 0 g Trans Fat, 0 mg Chol, 482 mg Sod, 37 g Carb, 8 g Fib, 9 g Prot, 60 mg Calc. **PointsPlus** value: **6.**

⏱ Time-Saver

For another speedy meal later in the week, double the bean mixture and refrigerate half in an airtight container up to 4 days.

Herbed Bean and Tomato Pita Pizzas

SERVES 4

1 (15½-ounce) can chickpeas, rinsed and drained

1 tablespoon extra-virgin olive oil

2 teaspoons chopped fresh thyme or ½ teaspoon dried

Pinch crushed red pepper

4 (7-inch) whole-wheat pita breads

1 cup fat-free ricotta cheese

12 cherry tomatoes, halved

¼ cup grated Parmesan cheese

1 Put a baking sheet on the middle rack of the oven and preheat the oven to 425°F.

2 Meanwhile, combine the chickpeas, oil, thyme, and crushed red pepper in a medium bowl and coarsely mash with a wooden spoon.

3 Spread one-fourth of the chickpea mixture on each pita; top each with ¼ cup of the ricotta, 6 tomato halves, and 1 tablespoon of the Parmesan. Place the pizzas on the preheated baking sheet and bake until the topping is heated through and the pitas are crisp, about 5 minutes.

Per serving (1 pizza): 386 Cal, 9 g Fat, 2 g Sat Fat, 0 g Trans Fat, 11 mg Chol, 558 mg Sod, 57 g Carb, 9 g Fib, 23 g Prot, 237 mg Calc. *PointsPlus* value: **9**.

⏱ Time-Saver

Substitute 1 (14 ½-ounce) can diced tomatoes, drained, for the halved cherry tomatoes.

Top: Mediterranean-Style Salad Pizzas (page 211); bottom: Herbed Bean and Tomato Pita Pizzas

Cuban-Style Black Beans and Rice

SERVES 4

½ cup quick-cooking
  brown rice

2 (15½-ounce) cans black beans,
  drained but not rinsed

1 tablespoon olive oil

1 red bell pepper, chopped

1 onion, chopped

2 large garlic cloves, minced

1 cup drained petite diced
  tomatoes

1½ teaspoons ground cumin

½ teaspoon dried oregano

1 tablespoon lime juice

½ teaspoon hot pepper sauce

1 Cook the rice according to the package directions, omitting the fat if desired; keep warm.

2 With a fork, coarsely mash 1 cup of the beans; set aside.

3 Heat the oil in a large saucepan over medium-high heat. Add the bell pepper, onion, and garlic; cook, stirring, until the vegetables are softened, about 4 minutes. Add the whole and mashed beans, the tomatoes with their juice, the cumin, and oregano; cook, stirring occasionally, until the mixture thickens slightly and the vegetables are very tender, about 10 minutes.

4 Add the lime juice and pepper sauce, stirring to mix well. Serve over the rice.

Per serving (1 cup bean mixture and ½ cup rice): 252 Cal, 5 g Fat, 1 g Sat Fat, 0 g Trans Fat, 0 mg Chol, 538 mg Sod, 45 g Carb, 10 g Fib, 9 g Prot, 77 mg Calc. **PointsPlus** value: **5.**

⏱ Time-Saver

Instead of squeezing limes to make juice, use 2 teaspoons balsamic or red-wine vinegar.

Mediterranean-Style Salad Pizzas

SERVES 4

1 heart of romaine lettuce, thinly sliced (about 3 cups)

1 large tomato, seeded and chopped

1 (8½-ounce) can quartered artichoke hearts, drained

1 cup canned cannellini (white kidney) beans, rinsed and drained

1 (7-ounce) jar roasted red pepper, drained and coarsely chopped

2 tablespoons balsamic vinegar

1½ tablespoons olive oil

¼ teaspoon black pepper

4 (7-inch) whole-wheat tortillas

8 tablespoons shredded fat-free mozzarella cheese

1 Preheat the oven to 450°F.

2 Meanwhile, toss together the lettuce, tomato, artichoke hearts, beans, roasted pepper, vinegar, oil, and black pepper in a medium bowl. Arrange the tortillas on a baking sheet. Top each tortilla with about 1¼ cups of the salad and sprinkle with 2 tablespoons of the mozzarella. Bake until the cheese melts and the lettuce wilts slightly, about 5 minutes.

Per serving (1 pizza): 277 Cal, 7 g Fat, 1 g Sat Fat, 0 g Trans Fat, 3 mg Chol, 710 mg Sod, 43 g Carb, 10 g Fib, 14 g Prot, 216 mg Calc. **PointsPlus** value: **7.**

Tomato, Avocado, and Black Bean Tacos

SERVES 6

1 tablespoon extra-virgin olive oil

1 onion, chopped

1 tablespoon taco or Mexican seasoning

1 (15½-ounce) can black beans, rinsed and drained

3 plum tomatoes, chopped

6 (6-inch) corn tortillas, warmed

2 cups thinly sliced romaine lettuce

½ small Hass avocado, halved, pitted, peeled, and diced

6 tablespoons prepared salsa

¼ cup light sour cream

1 Heat the oil in a large nonstick skillet over medium-high heat. Add the onion and taco seasoning; cook, stirring occasionally, until softened, about 4 minutes. Transfer to a large bowl. Add the beans and tomatoes; toss to combine.

2 Sprinkle the center of each tortilla with ⅓ cup of the lettuce and top with about ⅓ cup of the bean mixture, one-sixth of the avocado, 1 tablespoon of the salsa, and 2 teaspoons of the sour cream. Fold up the tortillas to enclose the filling.

Per serving (1 taco): 202 Cal, 7 g Fat, 2 g Sat Fat, 0 g Trans Fat, 4 mg Chol, 363 mg Sod, 30 g Carb, 6 g Fib, 7 g Prot, 104 mg Calc. **PointsPlus** value: **5.**

Warm Lentil Salad with Tahini Dressing

SERVES 4

1¼ cups dried green (French) lentils, sorted and rinsed

4 cups water

2 lemons

1 tablespoon tahini

½ teaspoon salt

½ teaspoon black pepper

6 ounces low-fat firm tofu, cut into small dice

2 plum tomatoes, chopped

4 scallions, thinly sliced

1 Combine the lentils and water in a medium saucepan and bring to a boil over medium-high heat. Reduce the heat and simmer, covered, until the lentils are tender but still hold their shape, about 12 minutes; drain and set aside.

2 Meanwhile, grate the zest from one of the lemons into a serving bowl; add the juice of both lemons. Add the tahini, salt, and pepper; whisk until well combined. Add the remaining ingredients and toss to combine. Pour the dressing over the lentil mixture and toss gently to coat evenly.

Per serving (1 cup): 238 Cal, 3 g Fat, 0 g Sat Fat, 0 g Trans Fat, 0 mg Chol, 354 mg Sod, 38 g Carb, 10 g Fib, 18 g Prot, 68 mg Calc. **PointsPlus** value: **6.**

◆ Filling Extra

Add more flavor and color to this delicious salad by stirring 2 shredded carrots and half of a diced English (seedless) cucumber into the lentil mixture.

White Bean Bruschetta with Chopped Salad

SERVES 4

16 thin slices Italian bread
(4 ounces)

3 tomatoes, chopped

1 cucumber, peeled and
chopped

1 (8½-ounce) can quartered
artichoke hearts, drained and
coarsely chopped

4 tablespoons chopped pitted
green olives

2 tablespoons fat-free Italian
dressing

1 (15½-ounce) can small white
beans, rinsed and drained

¼ cup water

2 tablespoon lemon juice

1 tablespoon extra-virgin
olive oil

1 garlic clove

1 Preheat the oven to 400°F.

2 Arrange the slices of bread in a single layer on
a baking sheet; bake until lightly golden and crisp,
about 5 minutes. Set aside.

3 Meanwhile, to make the chopped salad, toss
together the tomatoes, cucumber, artichoke hearts,
olives, and dressing in a large bowl; set aside.

4 Combine the remaining ingredients in a
food processor and process until smooth. Spread
1 tablespoon of the bean mixture on each slice of
bread. Divide the salad evenly among 4 plates and
top each with 4 bruschetta.

Per serving (generous 1 cup salad and 4 bruschetta): 274 Cal,
6 g Fat, 1 g Sat Fat, 0 g Trans Fat, 0 mg Chol, 747 mg Sod,
44 g Carb, 10 g Fib, 13 g Prot, 135 mg Calc. *PointsPlus* value: **7.**

Spinach Fettuccine with Tomato-Soy Ragu

SERVES 4

1 (9-ounce) package fresh spinach fettuccine

1 tablespoon olive oil

1 onion, chopped

3 garlic cloves, minced

2 cups frozen soy protein crumbles

2 cups prepared fat-free tomato-basil sauce

½ teaspoon dried oregano

⅓ cup grated Parmesan cheese

1 Cook the fettuccine according to the package directions, omitting the salt if desired; drain and keep warm.

2 Meanwhile, heat the oil in a large nonstick skillet over medium-high heat. Add the onion and garlic; cook, stirring, until softened, about 4 minutes. Stir in the soy crumbles and cook, stirring, until heated through, about 3 minutes. Add the tomato sauce and oregano; reduce the heat and simmer until heated through, about 3 minutes.

3 Divide the pasta evenly among 4 plates; top evenly with the sauce and sprinkle with the Parmesan cheese.

Per serving (1 cup fettuccine, ¾ cup sauce, and generous tablespoon cheese): 370 Cal, 8 g Fat, 2 g Sat Fat, 0 g Trans Fat, 48 mg Chol, 753 mg Sod, 45 g Carb, 3 g Fib, 29 g Prot, 179 mg Calc. **PointsPlus** value: **9**.

Linguine with Creamy Roasted Pepper Sauce

SERVES 4

1 (9-ounce) package fresh linguine

1 teaspoon extra-virgin olive oil

1 small onion, chopped

2 garlic cloves, minced

¾ cup reduced-sodium vegetable broth

1 (12-ounce) jar roasted red pepper, drained and coarsely chopped

½ cup chopped fresh basil

⅛ teaspoon crushed red pepper

¼ cup fat-free half-and-half

1 Cook the linguine according to the package directions, omitting the salt if desired; drain. Transfer to a serving bowl and keep warm.

2 Meanwhile, heat the oil in a medium nonstick saucepan over medium heat. Add the onion and garlic; cook until softened, about 4 minutes. Stir in the broth, roasted pepper, basil, and crushed red pepper; cook, stirring occasionally, about 10 minutes. Remove the saucepan from the heat and stir in the half-and-half; let cool about 5 minutes.

3 Transfer the roasted pepper mixture to a blender or food processor and puree. Pour the sauce over the pasta and toss to coat evenly.

Per serving (1 cup linguine and ½ cup sauce): 258 Cal, 2 g Fat, 0 g Sat Fat, 0 g Trans Fat, 0 mg Chol, 244 mg Sod, 50 g Carb, 3 g Fib, 9 g Prot, 51 mg Calc. *PointsPlus* value: **6.**

Gnocchi with Herb-Walnut Pesto

SERVES 4

1 (17½-ounce) package fresh gnocchi

1 cup lightly packed flat-leaf parsley leaves

½ cup lightly packed fresh basil leaves

¼ cup grated Parmesan cheese

⅓ cup walnuts

2 tablespoons water

2 garlic cloves, peeled

½ teaspoon salt

¼ teaspoon black pepper

1 Cook the gnocchi according to the package directions, omitting the salt if desired; drain. Transfer to a serving bowl and keep warm.

2 Meanwhile, to make the pesto, combine the remaining ingredients in a blender and process until smooth. Spoon over the gnocchi and toss to coat.

Per serving (¾ cup): 295 Cal, 9 g Fat, 2 g Sat Fat, 0 g Trans Fat, 5 mg Chol, 868 mg Sod, 48 g Carb, 3 g Fib, 9 g Prot, 125 mg Calc. **PointsPlus** value: **8.**

Double Cheese and Macaroni

SERVES 4

1½ cups ditalini or small bow ties (farfalle)

1½ cups fat-free milk

1 tablespoon cornstarch

1 teaspoon mustard powder

¼ teaspoon black pepper

1 (14½-ounce) can diced tomatoes with green pepper and onion, drained

¾ cup shredded reduced-fat cheddar cheese

¾ cup shredded reduced-fat Monterey Jack cheese

Chopped fresh parsley (optional)

1 Cook the ditalini according to the package directions, omitting the salt if desired; drain and keep warm.

2 Meanwhile, whisk together the milk, cornstarch, mustard, and pepper in a large saucepan until smooth, then set over medium-high heat. Cook, stirring, until the sauce thickens and bubbles, about 4 minutes. Stir in the tomatoes and cook, stirring, until heated through, about 2 minutes. Add the cheddar and Monterey Jack; cook, stirring, just until melted. Stir in the pasta and cook until heated through, about 1 minute longer. Serve sprinkled with parsley, if using.

Per serving (1¼ cups): 322 Cal, 5 g Fat, 2 g Sat Fat, 0 g Trans Fat, 12 mg Chol, 703 mg Sod, 50 g Carb, 4 g Fib, 19 g Prot, 404 mg Calc. *PointsPlus* value: **8.**

Double Cheese and Macaroni

Orzo with Spring Vegetables and Ricotta

SERVES 4

1 cup orzo

½ pound asparagus, trimmed and cut into 1-inch pieces

1 cup frozen baby peas

1 tablespoon extra-virgin olive oil

1 red onion, thinly sliced

2 garlic cloves, minced

1 cup drained petite diced tomatoes

½ teaspoon salt

¼ teaspoon black pepper

1 cup fat-free ricotta cheese

¼ cup grated Parmesan cheese

¼ cup coarsely chopped fresh basil

1 Cook the orzo according to the package directions, omitting the salt if desired; add the asparagus and peas to the pot during the last 3 minutes of cooking time. Drain and keep warm.

2 Meanwhile, heat the oil in a large nonstick skillet over medium-high heat. Add the onion and garlic; cook, stirring, until softened, about 4 minutes. Add the tomatoes, orzo, asparagus, peas, salt, and pepper; cook until heated through, about 2 minutes. Remove the skillet from the heat and stir in the ricotta, Parmesan, and basil.

Per serving (1 ¼ cups): 306 Cal, 6 g Fat, 2 g Sat Fat, 0 g Trans Fat, 11 mg Chol, 691 mg Sod, 43 g Carb, 5 g Fib, 19 g Prot, 237 mg Calc. **PointsPlus** value: **6.**

◆ Filling Extra

Double the amount of asparagus.

Vegetable-Topped Orange Couscous

SERVES 4

¾ cup orange juice

½ cup water

¾ teaspoon salt

1 cup whole-wheat couscous

1 tablespoon olive oil

2 yellow squash, cut into
¼-inch slices

3 garlic cloves, sliced

1 teaspoon curry powder

1 (15½-ounce) can small white
beans, rinsed and drained

1 (14½-ounce) can diced
tomatoes with mushrooms and
garlic

2 scallions, sliced

1 Bring the orange juice, water, and ½ teaspoon of the salt to a boil in a small saucepan. Add the couscous; cover and remove from the heat. Let stand 5 minutes, then fluff with a fork. Set aside.

2 Meanwhile, heat the oil in a large nonstick skillet over medium-high heat. Add the squash, garlic, curry powder, and the remaining ¼ teaspoon salt. Cook, stirring frequently, until the squash is softened, about 5 minutes. Add the beans, the tomatoes with their juice, and the scallions; bring to a boil. Reduce the heat and simmer, stirring occasionally, about 5 minutes. Transfer the couscous to a serving bowl and spoon the vegetable mixture on top.

Per serving (¾ cup couscous and 1 ¼ cups vegetable mixture): 366 Cal, 7 g Fat, 1 g Sat Fat, 0 g Trans Fat, 0 mg Chol, 708 mg Sod, 67 g Carb, 11 g Fib, 16 g Prot, 128 mg Calc. **PointsPlus** value: **7.**

⏱ Time-Saver

Make the couscous up to 4 hours ahead and serve it at room temperature along with the vegetable mixture.

Couscous and Vegetable—Stuffed Tomatoes

SERVES 6

½ cup water

¾ teaspoon salt

⅓ cup whole-wheat couscous

6 large tomatoes

1 tablespoon extra-virgin
olive oil

1 zucchini, cut into ¼-inch dice

1 small red onion, chopped

1 (15½-ounce) can cannellini
(white kidney) beans, rinsed
and drained

1 (8-ounce) can no-salt-added
tomato sauce

⅓ cup crumbled fat-free
feta cheese

1 Bring the water and ¼ teaspoon of the salt to a boil in a small saucepan. Add the couscous; cover and remove from the heat. Let stand 5 minutes, then fluff with a fork. Set aside.

2 Meanwhile, cut a thin slice from the top of each tomato and reserve. With a spoon, carefully scoop out and discard the seeds and pulp.

3 Heat the oil in a large nonstick skillet over medium-high heat. Add the zucchini and onion; cook, stirring, until crisp-tender, about 4 minutes. Add the beans and tomato sauce; cook until the sauce slightly thickens, about 2 minutes. Remove the skillet from the heat and stir in the couscous, feta, and the remaining ½ teaspoon salt. Spoon ¾ cup of the filling into each tomato shell and cover with the reserved tomato tops.

Per serving (1 stuffed tomato): 178 Cal, 3 g Fat, 1 g Sat Fat, 0 g Trans Fat, 3 mg Chol, 429 mg Sod, 30 g Carb, 7 g Fib, 9 g Prot, 110 mg Calc. **PointsPlus** value: **4.**

⏱ Time-Saver

Use a grapefruit spoon to quickly remove the seeds and pulp from the tomatoes in step 2.

Double Cheese Polenta with Golden Onions

SERVES 6

1 tablespoon unsalted butter

4 onions, thinly sliced

1 tablespoon sugar

1 teaspoon salt

3 cups low-fat (1%) milk

2 cups water

¼ teaspoon black pepper

1 cup quick-cooking polenta

¾ cup crumbled blue cheese

2 ounces light cream cheese
(Neufchâtel)

⅓ cup chopped walnuts
(optional)

1 Melt the butter in a large nonstick skillet over medium-high heat. Add the onions, sugar, and ¼ teaspoon of the salt; cook, stirring occasionally, until golden, about 10 minutes.

2 Meanwhile, combine the milk, water, the remaining ¾ teaspoon salt, and the pepper in a medium saucepan; bring to a boil over high heat. Whisk in the polenta in a slow, steady stream; cook, whisking constantly, until thickened and smooth, about 5 minutes.

3 Remove the saucepan from the heat and add the blue cheese and cream cheese, stirring until melted and smooth. Spoon the polenta evenly into 4 shallow soup bowls. Top evenly with the onions and sprinkle with the walnuts, if using.

Per serving (¾ cup polenta and about ¼ cup onions without walnuts): 285 Cal, 11 g Fat, 7 g Sat Fat, 0 g Trans Fat, 30 mg Chol, 734 mg Sod, 36 g Carb, 2 g Fib, 12 g Prot, 265 mg Calc. *PointsPlus* value: **8.**

Asian Vegetables in Coconut Curry

SERVES 4

¾ cup light coconut milk

1 tablespoon Asian fish sauce

1 tablespoon packed brown
sugar

2 teaspoons cornstarch

½ teaspoon Thai red curry paste

3 teaspoons canola oil

1 (14-ounce) container low-fat
firm tofu, drained and cut into
½-inch cubes

¾ pound snow peas, trimmed
and halved on the diagonal

½ pound shiitake mushrooms,
stemmed, caps halved

2 red bell peppers, cut into strips

1 tablespoon grated peeled
fresh ginger

¼ cup water

1 Stir together the coconut milk, fish sauce, brown sugar, cornstarch, and curry paste in a small bowl until smooth; set aside.

2 Heat 1½ teaspoons of the oil in a large nonstick skillet over high heat. Add the tofu and cook, stirring often, until lightly golden, about 4 minutes; transfer to a small bowl.

3 Heat the remaining 1½ teaspoons oil in the skillet. Add the remaining ingredients; cook, stirring constantly, until the liquid evaporates and the vegetables are crisp-tender, about 3 minutes. Add the tofu and coconut milk mixture. Cook, stirring constantly, until the sauce thickens and bubbles, about 1 minute.

Per serving (about 1½ cups): 157 Cal, 7 g Fat, 3 g Sat Fat, 0 g Trans Fat, 0 mg Chol, 457 mg Sod, 18 g Carb, 3 g Fib, 11 g Prot, 67 mg Calc. **PointsPlus** value: **6.**

⏱ Time-Saver

Use an 8-ounce package of sliced cremini mushrooms in place of the shiitakes.

Mixed Vegetable and Tofu Stir-Fry

SERVES 4

¼ cup reduced-sodium soy sauce

2 tablespoons unseasoned rice vinegar

1 tablespoon honey

2 teaspoons cornstarch

1 teaspoon Asian (dark) sesame oil

1 onion, thinly sliced

2 garlic cloves, minced

1 (1-pound) bag fresh vegetables for stir-fry

1 yellow bell pepper, cut into strips

4 scallions, cut into 1½-inch lengths

1 (14-ounce) container firm tofu, drained and cut into ½-inch cubes

2 cups hot cooked quick-cooking brown rice

1 Stir together the soy sauce, vinegar, honey, and cornstarch in a small bowl until smooth; set aside.

2 Heat the sesame oil in a nonstick wok or large deep nonstick skillet over medium-high heat. When a drop of water sizzles in it, add the onion and garlic; stir-fry about 1 minute. Add the stir-fry vegetables, bell pepper, and scallions; stir-fry until crisp-tender, about 3 minutes. Add the tofu and stir-fry until heated through, about 2 minutes. Add the soy sauce mixture and stir-fry until the sauce thickens and bubbles, about 1 minute longer. Serve with the rice.

Per serving (about 1 ⅓ cups tofu mixture and ½ cup rice): 275 Cal, 7 g Fat, 1 g Sat Fat, 0 g Trans Fats, 0 mg Chol, 561 mg Sod, 43 g Carb, 8 g Fib, 15 g Prot, 267 mg Calc. *PointsPlus* value: **7.**

⏱ Time-Saver

Instead of cooking brown rice, microwave an 8.8-ounce package shelf-stable cooked brown rice according to the package directions. It will be ready in just 90 seconds.

Brown Rice and Soy Burritos

SERVES 4

¾ cup quick-cooking brown rice

2 teaspoons olive oil

1 red onion, sliced

1½ cups frozen soy protein crumbles

1 tablespoon pickled jalapeño peppers, chopped

1 tablespoon ground cumin

½ teaspoon salt

½ cup chopped fresh cilantro

¾ cup prepared fat-free salsa

4 tablespoons fat-free sour cream

4 (8-inch) whole-wheat tortillas, warmed

1 Prepare the rice according to the package directions, omitting the fat; keep warm.

2 Meanwhile, heat the oil in a large nonstick skillet over high heat. Add the onion and cook, stirring, until softened, about 4 minutes. Add the soy crumbles, jalapeños, cumin, and salt; cook, stirring, until heated through, about 3 minutes. Stir in the rice and cook about 1 minute longer. Stir in the cilantro.

3 Spoon one-fourth of the rice mixture, 3 tablespoons of the salsa, and 1 tablespoon of the sour cream on the center of each tortilla. Fold the bottom of each tortilla over the filling, then fold in the sides and roll up jelly-roll style.

Per serving (1 burrito): 358 Cal, 6 g Fat, 1 g Sat Fat, 0 g Trans Fat, 1 mg Chol, 849 mg Sod, 41 g Carb, 7 g Fib, 38 g Prot, 123 mg Calc. **PointsPlus** value: **9.**

Hunan-Style Vegetables and Tempeh

SERVES 4

1 cup vegetable broth

¼ cup hoisin sauce

1 tablespoon reduced-sodium
   soy sauce

2 teaspoons cornstarch

2 teaspoons canola oil

1 (8-ounce) package tempeh, cut
   into ½-inch cubes

1 tablespoon very thinly sliced
   peeled fresh ginger

1 (12-ounce) bag fresh
   vegetables for stir-fry

1 (8-ounce) container sliced
   white mushrooms

¼ teaspoon crushed red pepper

2 cups hot cooked quick-cooking
   brown rice

1 Stir together the broth, hoisin, soy sauce, and cornstarch in a small bowl until smooth; set aside.

2 Heat 1 teaspoon of the oil in a nonstick wok or large deep nonstick skillet over high heat. When a drop of water sizzles in it, add the tempeh and stir-fry until lightly browned, about 3 minutes. Transfer to a plate.

3 Heat the remaining 1 teaspoon oil in the wok. Add the ginger and stir-fry until fragrant, about 30 seconds. Add the stir-fry vegetables, mushrooms, and crushed red pepper; stir-fry until crisp-tender, about 3 minutes. Stir the broth mixture and add to the wok; stir-fry until the sauce thickens and bubbles, about 1 minute. Return the tempeh to the wok; stir-fry until heated through, about 1 minute longer. Serve with the rice.

Per serving (1 cup tempeh mixture and ½ cup rice): 445 Cal, 13 g Fat, 3 g Sat Fat, 0 g Trans Fat, 0 mg Chol, 864 mg Sod, 48 g Carb, 10 g Fib, 15 g Prot, 110 mg Calc. **PointsPlus** value: **9.**

Spanish Potato Tortilla

SERVES 4

6 large eggs

6 egg whites

½ teaspoon salt

¼ teaspoon black pepper

1 green bell pepper, chopped

1 small onion, chopped

1 (14½-ounce) can sliced
potatoes, rinsed and drained

½ teaspoon paprika, preferably
smoked

1 Preheat the broiler.

2 Beat the eggs, egg whites, salt, and black pepper in a large bowl.

3 Spray a large cast-iron or other heavy ovenproof skillet with olive oil nonstick spray and set over medium heat. Add the bell pepper and onion; cook, stirring, until softened, about 4 minutes. Add the potatoes, breaking up the larger slices with a wooden spoon. Sprinkle with the paprika.

4 Pour the egg mixture over the vegetables and cook until almost set, about 4 minutes, frequently lifting the edges with a heatproof rubber spatula to allow the uncooked portion of egg to run underneath. Place the skillet under the broiler about 5 inches from the heat and broil until the eggs are set and the top is lightly browned, 2–3 minutes. Cut into 4 wedges.

Per serving (1 wedge): 203 Cal, 8 g Fat, 3 g Sat Fat, 0 g Trans Fat, 318 mg Chol, 938 mg Sod, 15 g Carb, 3 g Fib, 17 g Prot, 56 mg Calc. *PointsPlus* value: **5.**

⏱ Time-Saver

Instead of taking the time to crack and separate the eggs for this dish, use 2¼ cups fat-free egg substitute.

Microwave Vegetable Strata

SERVES 4

4 cups small broccoli florets

1 red bell pepper, cut into
¾-inch pieces

1 zucchini, cut into ¾-inch pieces

1 cup packaged matchstick-cut
carrots

1 garlic clove, minced

½ teaspoon salt

4 slices whole-wheat bread, cut
into ½-inch pieces

2 large eggs

½ cup fat-free milk

1 teaspoon Dijon mustard

⅛ teaspoon black pepper

1 cup shredded fat-free cheddar
cheese

¼ cup grated Parmesan cheese

1 Combine the broccoli, bell pepper, zucchini, carrots, garlic, and ¼ teaspoon of the salt in a large microwavable bowl. Cover and microwave on High, stirring once, until crisp-tender, about 4 minutes; pour off any liquid and set aside.

2 Spray a microwavable 2-quart shallow baking dish with nonstick spray. Spread the pieces of bread in the dish. Beat the eggs, milk, mustard, black pepper, and remaining ¼ teaspoon salt in a bowl.

3 Spoon half of the vegetables on top of the bread; sprinkle with ½ cup of the cheddar and 2 tablespoons of the Parmesan. Top with the remaining vegetables. Pour the egg mixture on top. Sprinkle with the remaining ½ cup cheddar and 2 tablespoons Parmesan.

4 Cover and microwave on High 5 minutes. Uncover and cook at 50 percent power 4 minutes. Microwave on High until a knife inserted into the center comes out clean, about 2 minutes longer. Let stand 2 minutes before serving.

Per serving (about 1 ¾ cups): 255 Cal, 6 g Fat, 3 g Sat Fat, 0 g Trans Fat, 116 mg Chol, 994 mg Sod, 29 g Carb, 6 g Fib, 21 g Prot, 461 mg Calc. **PointsPlus** value: **6.**

Ricotta and Cheddar Cheese Omelette

SERVES 4

4 large eggs

4 egg whites

¾ teaspoon salt

¼ teaspoon black pepper

4 teaspoons olive oil

1 small red onion, chopped

½ cup chopped red bell pepper

1 teaspoon garlic and herb
   seasoning

¼ cup fat-free ricotta cheese

¼ cup shredded fat-free cheddar
   cheese

1 Lightly beat the eggs, egg whites, ½ teaspoon of the salt, and ⅛ teaspoon of the black pepper in a medium bowl; set aside.

2 Heat 2 teaspoons of the oil in a large nonstick skillet over medium heat. Add the onion, bell pepper, garlic and herb seasoning, and the remaining ¼ teaspoon salt and ⅛ teaspoon black pepper; cook, stirring, until the vegetables are softened, about 4 minutes. Transfer to a medium bowl and stir in the ricotta and cheddar.

3 Wipe the skillet clean with a paper towel. Add the remaining 2 teaspoons oil to the skillet and set over medium-high heat. Add the egg mixture and cook until almost set, about 3 minutes, frequently lifting the edges with a heatproof rubber spatula to allow the uncooked portion of egg to run underneath. Spoon the cheese mixture on one half of the eggs and fold the unfilled portion of egg over to enclose the filling. Cook, turning once, until the filling is heated through, about 2 minutes. Cut the omelette into 4 portions.

Per serving (¼ of omelette): 177 Cal, 10 g Fat, 2 g Sat Fat, 0 g Trans Fat, 215 mg Chol, 658 mg Sod, 7 g Carb, 1 g Fib, 14 g Prot, 128 mg Calc. **PointsPlus** value: **4.**

Scrambled Eggs with Zucchini and Scallions

SERVES 4

4 large eggs

4 egg whites

½ teaspoon salt

¼ teaspoon black pepper

1 tablespoon extra-virgin
   olive oil

1 zucchini, diced

3 scallions, chopped

1 garlic clove, minced

1 Lightly beat the eggs, egg whites, ¼ teaspoon of the salt, and ⅛ teaspoon of the pepper in a medium bowl; set aside.

2 Heat the oil in a large nonstick skillet over medium heat. Add the zucchini, scallions, garlic, and the remaining ¼ teaspoon salt and ⅛ teaspoon pepper; cook, stirring, until the vegetables are softened, about 5 minutes.

3 Add the egg mixture and cook until almost set, about 3 minutes, frequently lifting the edges with a heatproof rubber spatula to allow the uncooked portion of egg to run underneath.

Per serving (about ¾ cup): 137 Cal, 9 g Fat, 2 g Sat Fat, 0 g Trans Fat, 212 mg Chol, 413 mg Sod, 4 g Carb, 1 g Fib, 10 g Prot, 36 mg Calc. **PointsPlus** value: **3.**

⏱ Time-Saver

Use ¼ cup frozen chopped chives instead of the scallions.

Filet Mignon with Herb Butter

SERVES 4

4 teaspoons butter, softened

1 teaspoon chopped fresh thyme

1 teaspoon chopped fresh tarragon

1 teaspoon chopped chives

1 teaspoon grated lemon zest

¾ teaspoon salt

4 (3-ounce) filets mignons, ½ inch thick, trimmed

⅛ teaspoon black pepper

1 With a fork, mash together the butter, thyme, tarragon, chives, lemon zest, and ¼ teaspoon of the salt in a cup; set aside.

2 Sprinkle the beef with the remaining ½ teaspoon salt and the pepper. Spray a large nonstick skillet with nonstick spray; set over medium-high heat. Add the beef; cook until an instant-read thermometer inserted into the side of a steak registers 145°F for medium, about 4 minutes on each side. Transfer to a platter and top each steak with one-fourth of the herb butter.

Per serving (1 steak and about 1 teaspoon butter): 161 Cal, 9 g Fat, 4 g Sat Fat, 0 g Trans Fat, 45 mg Chol, 467 mg Sod, 0 g Carb, 0 g Fib, 18 g Prot, 8 mg Calc. **PointsPlus** value: **4.**

◆ Filling Extra

Serve with 2 cups of halved cherry tomatoes that have been cooked just until softened in a nonstick skillet.

Flank Steak with Herbes de Provence

SERVES 4

1½ tablespoons herbes de Provence

1 teaspoon salt

½ teaspoon black pepper

1 (1-pound) flank steak, trimmed

1 Combine the herbes de Provence, salt, and pepper in a small bowl. Rub the herb mixture on the steak.

2 Spray a large nonstick skillet or ridged grill pan with nonstick spray and set over medium-high heat. Place the steak in the skillet and cook until an instant-read thermometer inserted into the side of the steak registers 145°F for medium, about 5 minutes on each side.

3 Transfer the steak to a cutting board and let rest 5 minutes. Cut across the grain into 12 slices.

Per serving (3 slices steak): 206 Cal, 8 g Fat, 3 g Sat Fat, 0 g Trans Fats, 49 mg Chol, 632 mg Sod, 1 g Carb, 1 g Fib, 30 g Prot, 26 mg Calc. **PointsPlus** value: **5.**

Beef Skewers with Cilantro and Ginger

SERVES 4

¼ cup lightly packed fresh cilantro leaves

1 large garlic clove, peeled

4 quarter-size slices peeled fresh ginger

2 tablespoons water

2 teaspoons Asian (dark) sesame oil

1 pound boneless sirloin steak, trimmed and cut into long thin slices

16 cherry tomatoes

2 small zucchini, each cut crosswise into 8 pieces

2 cups cooked bulgur

1 Spray the rack of a broiler pan with nonstick spray and preheat the broiler.

2 Combine the cilantro, garlic, ginger, water, and sesame oil in a mini–food processor or blender and process until a paste forms.

3 Put the slices of steak in a large bowl. Add the cilantro paste and toss until the beef is coated. Thread the beef strips on 4 long metal skewers, piercing each strip in at least two places. Alternately thread the tomatoes and zucchini on 4 other long skewers. Place the skewers on the broiler rack and broil 5 inches from the heat until the beef is cooked through and the vegetables are crisp-tender, about 3 minutes on each side. Serve with the bulgur.

Per serving (1 beef skewer, 1 vegetable skewer, and ½ cup bulgur): 288 Cal, 7 g Fat, 2 g Sat Fat, 0 g Trans Fat, 73 mg Chol, 654 mg Sod, 23 g Carb, 6 g Fib, 34 g Prot, 33 mg Calc. **PointsPlus** value: **7.**

⏱ Time-Saver

Slash your prep time by buying sirloin steak that has already been trimmed and sliced for stir-frying.

Thai Beef and Lettuce Rolls

SERVES 4

1 pound ground lean beef
(7% fat or less)

4 garlic cloves, minced

1 tablespoon reduced-sodium
soy sauce

2 teaspoons chili garlic sauce

2 teaspoons packed brown sugar

1 teaspoon Asian (dark) sesame
oil

8 Boston lettuce leaves

1 cup packaged matchstick-cut
carrots

8 fresh cilantro sprigs

8 fresh mint sprigs

1 Mix together the ground beef, garlic, soy sauce, chili sauce, and brown sugar in a medium bowl until combined.

2 Spray a large nonstick skillet with nonstick spray and set over medium-high heat. Add the beef mixture and cook, breaking it apart with a wooden spoon, until browned, about 3 minutes. Stir in the sesame oil.

3 Place about ¼ cup of the beef mixture on each lettuce leaf. Top evenly with one-eighth of the carrots, 1 cilantro sprig, and 1 mint sprig. Fold in two opposite sides of each lettuce leaf.

Per serving (2 lettuce rolls): 195 Cal, 7 g Fat, 3 g Sat Fat, 0 g Trans Fat; 64 mg Chol, 228 mg Sod, 8 g Carb, 1 g Fib, 23 g Prot, 29 mg Calc. **PointsPlus** value: **5.**

⏱ Time-Saver

Use a ¼-cup dry measure to quickly and evenly divide the beef mixture in step 3.

Ginger Beef and Vegetable Fried Rice

SERVES 4

3 scallions, thinly sliced

1 tablespoon minced peeled
fresh ginger

2 garlic cloves, minced

½ pound ground lean beef
(7% fat or less)

1 (10-ounce) package frozen
mixed vegetables, thawed

2 cups cooked quick-cooking
brown rice

1 tablespoon reduced-sodium
soy sauce

2 teaspoons oyster sauce

2 teaspoons chili garlic sauce

1 Spray a nonstick wok or large deep nonstick skillet with nonstick spray and set over medium-high heat. Add the scallions, ginger, and garlic; stir-fry until fragrant, about 30 seconds. Add the ground beef and cook, breaking it apart with a wooden spoon, until browned, about 3 minutes.

2 Add the mixed vegetables and stir-fry about 2 minutes. Add the rice and stir-fry about 2 minutes. Add the soy sauce, oyster sauce, and chili sauce. Stir-fry until heated through, about 1 minute longer.

Per serving (1 ¼ cups): 226 Cal, 4 g Fat, 2 g Sat Fat, 0 g Trans Fat, 32 mg Chol, 688 mg Sod, 31 g Carb, 6 g Fib, 16 g Prot, 52 mg Calc. **PointsPlus** value: **5.**

⏱ Time-Saver

Replace the minced fresh ginger with a 1-inch piece of unpeeled ginger—the stir-fry will still have a taste of ginger, though less intense. Discard the piece of ginger before serving.

Double Mushroom Burgers with Spiced-up Ketchup

SERVES 4

1 ounce dried porcini
mushrooms

5 large cremini mushrooms,
halved

1 pound ground lean beef
(7% fat or less)

1 teaspoon salt

¼ teaspoon black pepper

2 tablespoons ketchup

½ teaspoon ground allspice

¼ teaspoon ground cloves

⅛ teaspoon garlic powder

4 whole-wheat hamburger buns

1 Put the dried and fresh mushrooms in a food processor and process until finely chopped; transfer to a medium bowl. Add the ground beef, salt, and pepper to the mushrooms; with damp hands, shape into 4 patties.

2 Spray a large nonstick skillet with olive oil nonstick spray and set over medium-high heat. Add the patties and cook until an instant-read thermometer inserted into the side of a burger registers 160°F, about 4 minutes on each side.

3 Meanwhile, mix together the remaining ingredients in a small bowl. Serve each burger in a bun with the spiced-up ketchup alongside.

Per serving (1 burger and scant 2 teaspoons ketchup mixture): 298 Cal, 8 g Fat, 3 g Sat Fat, 0 g Trans Fat, 64 mg Chol, 927 mg Sod, 26 g Carb, 4 g Fib, 29 g Prot, 64 mg Calc. *PointsPlus* value: **7**.

Pork Chops with Scallion-Lemon Relish

SERVES 4

8 scallions, finely chopped

2 tablespoons reduced-sodium soy sauce

2 teaspoons grated lemon zest

1 tablespoon lemon juice

4 (6-ounce) pork loin chops, trimmed

1 teaspoon salt

¼ teaspoon black pepper

1 Spray the rack of a broiler pan with olive oil nonstick spray and preheat the broiler.

2 Meanwhile, to make the relish, combine the scallions, soy sauce, and lemon zest and juice in a small bowl; set aside.

3 Sprinkle the pork chops with the salt and pepper. Place on the broiler rack and broil 4 inches from the heat until an instant-read thermometer inserted into the side of a chop registers 160°F for medium, about 6 minutes on each side. Serve with the relish.

Per serving (1 pork chop and 2 tablespoons relish): 212 Cal, 9 g Fat, 3 g Sat Fat, 0 g Trans Fat, 76 mg Chol, 907 mg Sod, 3 g Carb, 1 g Fib, 27 g Prot, 31 mg Calc. **PointsPlus** value: **6.**

Mustard-Coated Lamb Steaks

SERVES 4

2 tablespoons Dijon mustard

2 teaspoons herbes de Provence

2 garlic cloves, minced

1 teaspoon salt

½ teaspoon black pepper

2 (½-pound) leg of lamb steaks,
  trimmed

4 plum tomatoes, halved

1 Spray the rack of a broiler pan with olive oil nonstick spray and preheat the broiler.

2 Combine the mustard, herbes de Provence, garlic, ½ teaspoon of the salt, and ¼ teaspoon of the pepper in a cup. Brush the mixture on the steaks.

3 Place the steaks on the broiler rack. Place the tomatoes, cut side up, on the broiler rack around the steaks and sprinkle with the remaining ½ teaspoon salt and ¼ teaspoon pepper. Broil 4 inches from the heat until an instant-read thermometer inserted into the side of a steak registers 145°F for medium, about 6 minutes on each side, and the tomatoes are slightly softened, about 8 minutes. Cut each steak in half and serve with the tomatoes.

Per serving (½ lamb steak and 2 tomato halves): 129 Cal, 6 g Fat, 2 g Sat Fat, 0 g Trans Fat, 52 mg Chol, 374 mg Sod, 2 g Carb, 0 g Fib, 17 g Prot, 25 mg Calc. ***PointsPlus*** value: **5.**

Orange-Glazed Chicken Breasts

SERVES 4

½ cup orange preserves

2 scallions, chopped

1 tablespoon Dijon mustard

½ teaspoon salt

4 (5-ounce) skinless boneless chicken breast halves

1 Spray the rack of a broiler pan with nonstick spray and preheat the broiler.

2 Combine the preserves, scallions, mustard, and salt in a small bowl. Place the chicken on the broiler rack and brush with half of the preserve mixture. Broil 4 inches from the heat about 3 minutes. Turn the chicken and brush with the remaining preserve mixture; broil until lightly browned and cooked through, about 3 minutes longer.

Per serving (1 chicken breast half): 245 Cal, 3 g Fat, 1 g Sat Fat, 0 g Trans Fat, 72 mg Chol, 398 mg Sod, 27 g Carb, 2 g Fib, 27 g Prot, 37 mg Calc. **PointsPlus** value: **5.**

Sautéed Chicken with White Wine and Mushrooms

SERVES 4

4 (¼-pound) chicken breast cutlets

½ teaspoon salt

¼ teaspoon black pepper

1 tablespoon unsalted butter

½ pound sliced white mushrooms

2 garlic cloves, minced

¾ cup dry white wine

1 tablespoon chopped fresh rosemary

1 Sprinkle the chicken with ¼ teaspoon of the salt and the pepper. Spray a large nonstick skillet with nonstick spray and set over medium-high heat. Add the chicken and cook until browned and cooked through, about 5 minutes on each side. Transfer to a platter; keep warm.

2 Melt the butter in the skillet. Add the mushrooms, garlic, and the remaining ¼ teaspoon salt; cook, stirring, until the mushrooms are browned, about 3 minutes. Add the wine and rosemary; cook until most of the liquid evaporates, about 3 minutes longer. Spoon the mushroom sauce over the chicken.

Per serving (1 chicken cutlet and ¼ cup mushroom sauce): 189 Cal, 7 g Fat, 3 g Sat Fat, 0 g Trans Fat, 76 mg Chol, 363 mg Sod, 4 g Carb, 1 g Fib, 26 g Prot, 26 mg Calc. *PointsPlus* value: **6.**

◆ *Filling Extra*

Serve this saucy chicken on a bed of whole wheat spaghetti (1 cup cooked whole wheat spaghetti per serving will increase the *PointsPlus* value by **4**).

Chicken Burgers on Garlic Bread

SERVES 4

1 pound ground skinless chicken breast

2 tablespoons plain dried bread crumbs

2 tablespoons coarse-grained Dijon mustard

2 shallots, minced

1 teaspoon dried thyme

½ teaspoon salt

¼ teaspoon black pepper

1 (8-ounces) length of French bread, cut into 4 equal pieces and split

2 teaspoons olive oil

1 garlic clove, halved

1 Spray the rack of a broiler pan with nonstick spray and preheat the broiler.

2 Mix together the chicken, bread crumbs, mustard, shallots, thyme, salt, and pepper in a medium bowl until combined. With damp hands, shape into 4 (½-inch-thick) oval patties.

3 Place the patties on the broiler rack and broil 4 inches from the heat until an instant-read thermometer inserted into the side of a burger registers 165°F, 5–6 minutes on each side.

4 Meanwhile, brush the cut sides of the bread with the oil. Broil, cut side up, alongside the burgers until lightly toasted, about 3 minutes. Rub the cut side of the garlic over the toasted side of the bread. Place a burger on the bottom half of each piece of bread and cover with the top of the bread.

Per serving (1 burger): 353 Cal, 8 g Fat, 2 g Sat Fat, 0 g Trans Fat, 68 mg Chol, 938 mg Sod, 37 g Carb, 2 g Fib, 33 g Prot, 58 mg Calc. **PointsPlus** value: **9.**

◈ Filling Extra

Top each burger with ½ jarred roasted red pepper (not packed in oil) and a lettuce leaf or two.

Chicken Picadillo

SERVES 4

2 teaspoons olive oil

1 onion, finely chopped

3 garlic cloves, minced

½ pound ground skinless
chicken breast

½ teaspoon salt

¼ teaspoon ground cumin

¼ teaspoon black pepper

1 (15½-ounce) can red kidney
beans, rinsed and drained

1 (15-ounce) can crushed
tomatoes

¼ cup pimiento-stuffed olives,
coarsely chopped

1 Heat the oil in a large nonstick skillet over medium heat. Add the onion and garlic; cook, stirring, until softened, about 4 minutes. Add the chicken and cook, breaking it up with a wooden spoon, until no longer pink, about 4 minutes. Add the salt, cumin, and pepper; cook, stirring, about 30 seconds.

2 Add the remaining ingredients to the skillet and bring to a boil over medium-high heat. Reduce the heat and simmer until the liquid is slightly thickened, about 3 minutes.

Per serving (1 cup): 231 Cal, 6 g Fat, 1 g Sat Fat, 0 g Trans Fat, 34 mg Chol, 623 mg Sod, 25 g Carb, 7 g Fib, 20 g Prot, 82 mg Calc. *PointsPlus* value: **6.**

⏱ Time-Saver

Substitute 1 (14 ½-ounce) can fire-roasted crushed tomatoes for the regular crushed tomatoes and leave out the cumin.

Sliced Chicken and Smoked Mozzarella Salad

SERVES 4

¾ pound cooked skinless boneless chicken breast, sliced

3 ounces part-skim smoked mozzarella cheese, thinly sliced

¼ teaspoon black pepper

1 pint cherry tomatoes, halved

10 pitted kalamata olives

12 fresh basil leaves

Alternate the slices of chicken and mozzarella on a platter. Sprinkle with the pepper, then scatter the tomatoes, olives, and basil on top. Serve at once or refrigerate, covered, up to 3 hours.

Per serving (about 1 cup): 197 Cal, 8 g Fat, 4 g Sat Fat, 0 g Trans Fats, 63 mg Chol, 251 mg Sod, 5 g Carb, 2 g Fib, 25 g Prot, 186 mg Calc. *PointsPlus* value: **6.**

Currant and Walnut–Topped Turkey Cutlets

SERVES 4

4 (¼-pound) turkey breast cutlets

½ teaspoon salt

¼ teaspoon black pepper

1 teaspoon olive oil

¼ cup finely chopped walnuts

2 tablespoons currants

2 tablespoons plain dried bread crumbs

2 tablespoons grated Parmesan cheese

1 Preheat the broiler.

2 Sprinkle the turkey cutlets with the salt and pepper. Heat the oil in a large ovenproof skillet over medium-high heat. Add the turkey and cook until browned and cooked through, about 3 minutes on each side. Remove the skillet from the heat.

3 Meanwhile, combine the walnuts, currants, and bread crumbs in a small bowl. Sprinkle evenly over the turkey and sprinkle with the Parmesan. Place the skillet under the broiler 4 inches from the heat and broil until the topping is crispy, about 1 minute.

Per serving (1 turkey cutlet with topping): 219 Cal, 8 g Fat, 2 g Sat Fat, 0 g Trans Fat, 79 mg Chol, 394 mg Sod, 7 g Carb, 1 g Fib, 28 g Prot, 46 mg Calc. **PointsPlus** value: **5.**

⏱ Time-Saver

Instead of chopping the walnuts by hand, toss them into a mini–food processor and pulse until finely chopped—or purchase chopped walnuts.

Salmon with Balsamic-Honey Sauce

SERVES 4

½ cup balsamic vinegar

1 tablespoon honey

4 (¼-pound) salmon steaks

½ teaspoon salt

½ teaspoon black pepper

1 tablespoon olive oil

4 cups herb salad mix (about 6 ounces)

1 To make the sauce, combine the vinegar and honey in a small saucepan and bring to a boil over medium-high heat. Boil until reduced to about ¼ cup, about 4 minutes. Remove the saucepan from the heat and let cool.

2 Sprinkle the salmon with ¼ teaspoon of the salt and the pepper. Spray a large nonstick skillet or nonstick ridged grill pan with nonstick spray and set over medium-high heat. Add the salmon and cook until just opaque in the center, about 3 minutes on each side.

3 Meanwhile, whisk together the vinegar mixture, oil, and the remaining ¼ teaspoon salt in a small bowl. Divide the salad evenly among 4 plates; place a salmon steak on top of each salad and drizzle evenly with the sauce. Remove the salmon skin before eating.

Per serving (1 salmon steak, 1 cup herb salad, and scant 2 tablespoons sauce): 220 Cal, 10 g Fat, 2 g Sat Fat, 0 g Trans Fat, 74 mg Chol, 398 mg Sod, 7 g Carb, 2 g Fib, 25 g Prot, 61 mg Calc. **PointsPlus** value: **7.**

Microwave Salmon Fillet with Lemon Sauce

SERVES 4

1¼ pounds skinless salmon fillet, cut into 4 equal pieces

2 tablespoons lemon juice

¾ teaspoon salt

¼ teaspoon black pepper

2 tablespoons all-purpose flour

1 cup low-fat (1%) milk

1 teaspoon grated lemon zest

1 Spray a 2-quart microwavable dish with nonstick spray. Place the salmon fillets in the dish in a single layer and sprinkle with the lemon juice, salt, and pepper. Cover the dish with a piece of plastic wrap with a few holes poked in. Microwave on High until the salmon is just opaque in the center, 5–6 minutes; let stand, covered, about 1 minute. Transfer to a platter and keep warm. Pour the accumulated fish liquid into a glass measure and set aside.

2 Whisk together the flour and ¼ cup of the milk in a medium saucepan until smooth. Whisk in the remaining ¾ cup milk; add the lemon zest. Cook over medium heat, whisking constantly, until the sauce thickens and bubbles, about 3 minutes. Whisk in the reserved fish liquid and cook until heated through, about 1 minute longer. Spoon over the salmon.

Per serving (1 piece salmon and about ¼ cup sauce): 245 Cal, 9 g Fat, 3 g Sat Fat, 0 g Trans Fat, 96 mg Chol, 560 mg Sod, 7 g Carb, 0 g Fib, 33 g Prot, 98 mg Calc. ***PointsPlus*** value: **7.**

Salmon with Tomato-Scallion Relish

SERVES 4

4 large plum tomatoes, chopped

¼ cup coarsely chopped
flat-leaf parsley

2 scallions, chopped

2 garlic cloves, minced

1 teaspoon grated lemon zest

2 teaspoons lemon juice

¾ teaspoon salt

¼ teaspoon black pepper

4 (6-ounce) skinless salmon fillets

1 To make the relish, combine the tomatoes, parsley, scallions, garlic, lemon zest and juice, ½ teaspoon of the salt, and ⅛ teaspoon of the pepper in a small bowl; set aside.

2 Sprinkle the salmon with the remaining ¼ teaspoon salt and ⅛ teaspoon pepper. Spray a large nonstick skillet with olive oil nonstick spray and set over medium-high heat. Add the salmon and cook about 4 minutes. Turn and cook about 1 minute longer. Reduce the heat to medium and cook, covered, until the salmon is just opaque in the center, about 2 minutes longer. Serve with the tomato-scallion relish.

Per serving (1 piece salmon and about ⅓ cup relish): 259 Cal, 10 g Fat, 3 g Sat Fat, 0 g Trans Fat, 112 mg Chol, 550 mg Sod, 4 g Carb, 1 g Fib, 37 g Prot, 40 mg Calc. **PointsPlus** value: **7.**

Filling Extra

Make a double amount of this tasty tomato relish to enjoy with the fish.

Cajun Tuna with Scallion-Caper Mayonnaise

SERVES 4

½ cup fat-free mayonnaise

2 scallions, chopped

2 teaspoons capers, drained and chopped

2 teaspoons Dijon mustard

⅛ teaspoon black pepper

1 tablespoon Cajun seasoning

4 (6-ounce) tuna steaks

2 teaspoons canola oil

1 Combine the mayonnaise, scallions, capers, mustard, and pepper in a serving dish; set aside.

2 Sprinkle the Cajun seasoning on the tuna steaks. Heat the oil in a large nonstick skillet over medium-high heat. Add the tuna and cook until medium-rare, about 2 minutes on each side. Serve with the mayonnaise.

Per serving (1 tuna steak and about 3 tablespoons mayonnaise): 266 Cal, 12 g Fat, 3 g Sat Fat, 0 g Trans Fat, 104 mg Chol, 842 mg Sod, 5 g Carb, 1 g Fib, 33 g Prot, 28 mg Calc. *PointsPlus* value: **7.**

Skillet Shrimp with Onion, Succotash, and Tomatoes

SERVES 4

1½ teaspoons olive oil

1 pound peeled and deveined medium shrimp

1 red onion, chopped

1 (10-ounce) package frozen succotash

1 (14½-ounce) can petite diced tomatoes, drained

½ teaspoon salt

¼ teaspoon black pepper

12 large fresh basil leaves, thinly sliced

1 Heat 1 teaspoon of the oil in a large nonstick skillet over medium-high heat. Add the shrimp and cook just until opaque in the center, about 2 minutes on each side. Transfer to a medium bowl and keep warm.

2 Add the remaining ½ teaspoon oil, the onion, succotash, tomatoes, salt, and pepper to the skillet. Cook, stirring, until the onion softens, about 4 minutes. Return the shrimp to the skillet along with the basil. Cook, stirring, until heated through, about 1 minute.

Per serving (about 1½ cups): 165 Cal, 3 g Fat, 1 g Sat Fat, 0 Trans Fats, 161 mg Chol, 592 mg Sod, 16 g Carb, 3 g Fib, 20 g Prot, 64 mg Calc. ***PointsPlus*** value: **5.**

Time-Saver

To slice the basil in a flash, stack the leaves and tightly roll them up from one long side, jelly-roll style, then cut into thin slices.

Potato Pierogies with Wild Mushroom Sauce

SERVES 4

1 teaspoon olive oil

2 cups sliced mixed mushrooms, such as white, oyster, and cremini

½ teaspoon dried thyme

½ teaspoon salt

¼ teaspoon black pepper

1 tablespoon all-purpose flour

⅔ cup low-fat (1%) milk

¼ cup reduced-sodium vegetable broth

1 (1-pound) package frozen low-fat potato pierogies, thawed

2 tablespoons light sour cream

1 Heat the oil in a large nonstick skillet over medium-high heat. Add the mushrooms, thyme, salt, and pepper; cook, stirring, until tender and lightly browned, about 4 minutes.

2 Sprinkle the flour over the mushroom mixture, stirring to combine. Gradually add the milk and broth, stirring until smooth. Add the pierogies and bring to a boil. Remove the skillet from the heat and stir in the sour cream.

Per serving (about 1½ cups): 233 Cal, 5 g Fat, 1 g Sat Fat, 0 g Trans Fat, 10 mg Chol, 674 mg Sod, 39 g Carb, 3 g Fib, 9 g Prot, 61 mg Calc. **PointsPlus** value: **6.**

⏱ Time-Saver

Double the recipe and save half for another speedy meal. Let the reserved half cool completely, then refrigerate in an airtight container up to 4 days.

Double Chocolate–
Cranberry Pudding

Sweet Sensations

Fruit-Filled Crêpes with
Brown Sugar—Sour Cream

Sautéed Bananas with
Rum and Brown Sugar

Berry-Topped Cake
with Strawberry Sauce

Cinnamon-Sugared Pineapple
with Coconut Sorbet

Orange-Poached Figs
with Yogurt and Pistachios

One-Step Fruit Fool

Fresh Fruit with Ricotta Cream

Creamy Brown Rice and
Dried Cherry Pudding

Vanilla Yogurt and
Anisette-Toast Parfaits

Double Chocolate—Cranberry Pudding

Cold Crenshaw Melon Soup
with Honey and Mint

Fresh Fruit Gazpacho

Five Fruit Salad

Watermelon Salad
with Mint and Lime

Tropical Fruit Salad
with Toasted Coconut

Strawberry-Vanilla Malted

Peach-Strawberry Milk Shakes

Chocolate-Raspberry Cooler

Microwave Spiced
Popcorn—Dried Fruit Mix

Fruit-Filled Crêpes with Brown Sugar–Sour Cream

SERVES 4

¼ cup light sour cream

2 tablespoons packed dark brown sugar

12 strawberries, hulled and halved

1 (6-ounce) container blackberries

2 tablespoons orange juice

4 (9-inch) ready-to-use crêpes

1 Combine the sour cream and 1 tablespoon of the brown sugar in a small bowl; set aside.

2 Combine the strawberries, blackberries, orange juice, and the remaining 1 tablespoon brown sugar in a medium nonstick skillet and set over high heat. Cook until the berries are slightly softened, about 2 minutes.

3 Place 1 crêpe on each of 4 plates. Spoon ½ cup of the fruit mixture down the center of each crêpe. Fold one edge of the crêpe over the filling, then fold in the two opposite sides. Roll the crêpe up jelly-roll style to enclose the filling. Top evenly with the remaining fruit mixture and 1 tablespoon of the sour cream mixture.

Per serving (1 filled crêpe): 192 Cal, 5 g Fat, 2 g Sat Fat, 1 g Trans Fat, 38 mg Chol, 188 mg Sod, 34 g Carb, 2 g Fib, 6 g Prot, 92 mg Calc. *PointsPlus* value: **5.**

Fruit-Filled Crêpes with Brown Sugar–Sour Cream

Sautéed Bananas with Rum and Brown Sugar

SERVES 4

4 medium-ripe bananas, peeled

2 teaspoons unsalted butter

¼ cup packed dark brown sugar

3 tablespoons dark rum

½ teaspoon cinnamon

1 teaspoon vanilla extract

1 pint vanilla fat-free frozen yogurt

1 Cut the bananas crosswise in half, then cut each piece lengthwise in half.

2 Melt the butter in a large nonstick skillet over medium heat. Add the bananas, cut side down, and cook until golden brown, about 1½ minutes on each side. Add the brown sugar, dark rum, and cinnamon; cook until the sugar is dissolved and the mixture is syrupy, about 1 minute. Stir in the vanilla.

3 Place a ½-cup scoop of the frozen yogurt in each of 4 ice-cream dishes. Top each with 4 pieces of banana and about 2 tablespoons of the sauce. Serve at once.

Per serving (1 dish): 295 Cal, 2 g Fat, 1 g Sat Fat, 0 g Trans Fat, 7 mg Chol, 74 mg Sod, 64 g Carb, 3 g Fib, 5 g Prot, 182 mg Calc. **PointsPlus** value: **9.**

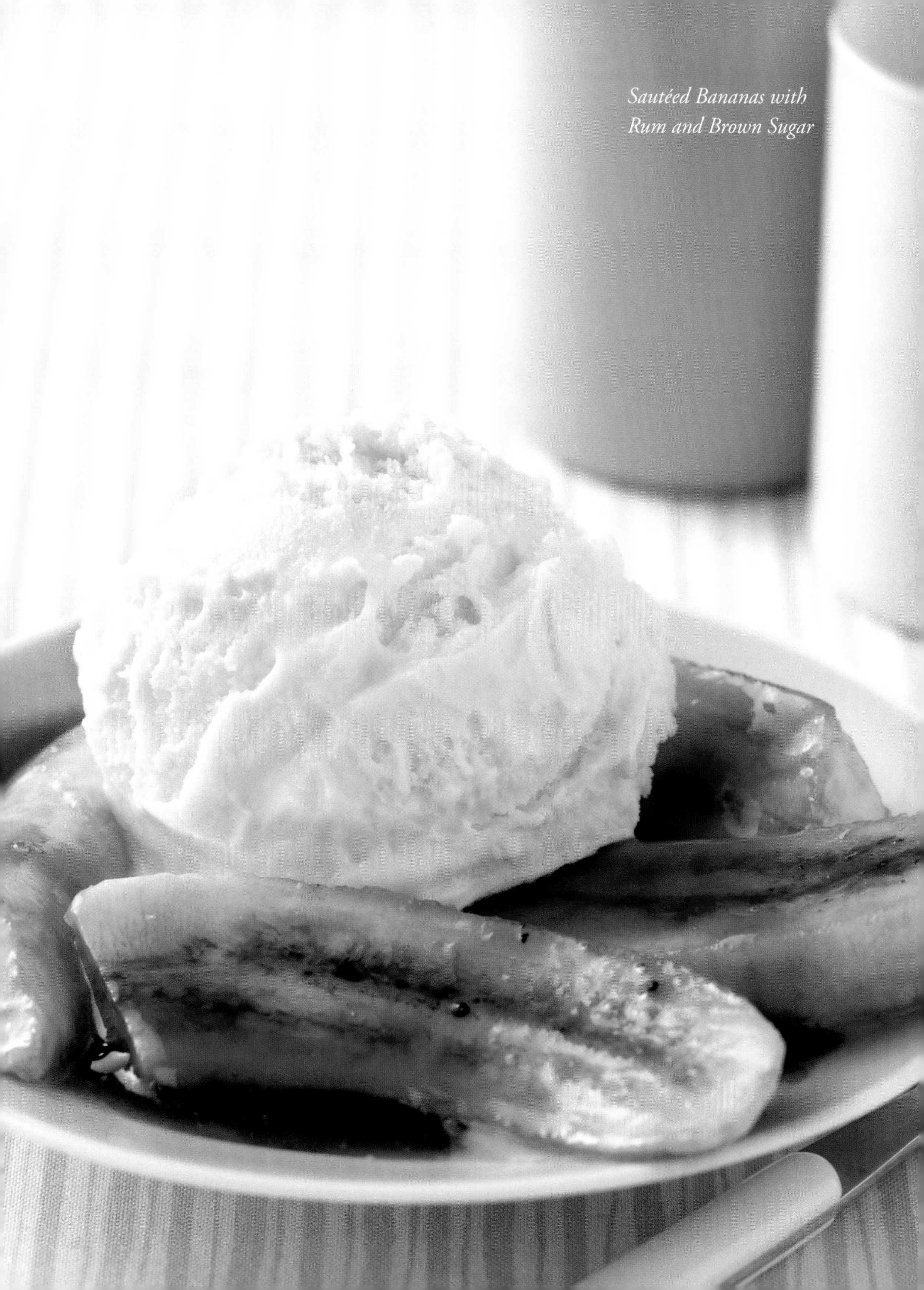

Sautéed Bananas with Rum and Brown Sugar

Berry-Topped Cake with Strawberry Sauce

SERVES 6

2 (6-ounce) containers raspberries

2 (6-ounce) containers blackberries

2 tablespoons thinly sliced fresh mint

½ cup + 2 tablespoons sugar

1 tablespoon + 2 teaspoons lime juice

2 cups strawberries, hulled

1 (9-ounce) store-bought angel food cake, cut into 6 wedges

1 Gently toss together the raspberries, blackberries, mint, 2 tablespoons of the sugar, and 2 teaspoons of the lime juice in a large bowl; set aside.

2 Combine the strawberries and the remaining ½ cup sugar and 1 tablespoon lime juice in a blender or food processor and puree.

3 Place a wedge of cake on each of 6 plates. Spoon about 3 tablespoons of the strawberry sauce around each wedge and top with about ⅔ cup of the berry mixture.

Per serving (1 plate): 275 Cal, 1 g Fat, 0 g Sat Fat, 0 g Trans Fat, 0 mg Chol, 321 mg Sod, 66 g Carb, 5 g Fib, 4 g Prot, 33 mg Calc. **PointsPlus** value: **6.**

⏱ Time-Saver

To save time hulling fresh strawberries, use frozen whole unsweetened strawberries and there's no need to thaw them before pureeing.

Cinnamon-Sugared Pineapple with Coconut Sorbet

SERVES 4

3 tablespoons sugar

½ teaspoon cinnamon

Pinch black pepper

1 precut fresh pineapple, sliced and cut into wedges

1⅓ cups coconut sorbet

4 tablespoons sliced almonds, toasted

2 tablespoons chopped fresh cilantro

1 Combine the sugar, cinnamon, and pepper in a cup. Put the pineapple in a large bowl; sprinkle with the cinnamon sugar and toss to coat evenly.

2 Divide the pineapple evenly among 4 dessert dishes. Top each serving with ⅓-cup scoop of the sorbet, 1 tablespoon of the almonds, and ½ tablespoon of the cilantro. Serve at once.

Per serving (1 dish): 228 Cal, 5 g Fat, 2 g Sat Fat, 0 g Trans Fat, 1 mg Chol, 20 mg Sod, 47 g Carb, 3 g Fib, 2 g Prot, 36 mg Calc. **PointsPlus** value: **6.**

◆ Filling Extra

Add 2 sliced large bananas to the pineapple in step 1.

One-Step Fruit Fool

SERVES 4

1 (8-ounce) container frozen fat-free whipped topping, thawed

3 tablespoons strawberry preserves

3 tablespoons orange preserves

Divide the whipped topping evenly between 2 small bowls. With a rubber spatula, gently fold the strawberry preserves into the whipped topping in one bowl and the orange preserves into topping in the other bowl. Spoon the strawberry mixture evenly into 4 glass dishes, then spoon the apricot mixture evenly on top.

Per serving (about 1 cup): 147 Cal, 1 g Fat, 1 g Sat Fat, 0 g Trans Fat, 0 mg Chol, 35 mg Sod, 36 g Carb, 1 g Fib, 0 g Prot, 6 mg Calc. *PointsPlus* value: **4.**

◆ *Filling Extra*

Serve each fool topped with ¼ cup fresh or thawed frozen raspberries.

Fresh Fruit with Ricotta Cream

SERVES 2

3 cups mixed fruit, such as diced mango, raspberries, halved strawberries, and sliced kiwi fruit

Grated zest of ½ orange

3 tablespoons orange juice

¼ cup part-skim ricotta cheese

1½ tablespoons confectioners' sugar

¼ teaspoon vanilla extract

1 Combine the fruit and orange zest and juice in a small bowl. Spoon 1½ cups of the fruit mixture into each of 2 dessert dishes.

2 Combine the ricotta, confectioners' sugar, and vanilla in a blender or food processor and puree. Spoon 1½ tablespoons of the ricotta mixture on top of each serving.

Per serving (1 dish): 162 Cal, 3 g Fat, 2 g Sat Fat, 0 g Trans Fats, 9 mg Chol, 56 mg Sod, 30 g Carb, 5 g Fib, 6 g Prot, 114 mg Calc. *PointsPlus* value: **5.**

Creamy Brown Rice and Dried Cherry Pudding

SERVES 6

2 cups cooked quick-cooking
brown rice

1½ cups reduced-fat (2%) milk

½ cup sugar

½ cup dried cherries or golden
raisins

½ teaspoon almond extract

¼ teaspoon cinnamon

Pinch nutmeg

1 Combine the rice, milk, sugar, and dried cherries in a medium saucepan and bring to a boil over high heat. Reduce the heat and simmer, stirring occasionally, until slightly thickened, about 5 minutes.

2 Remove the saucepan from the heat; stir in the almond extract, cinnamon, and nutmeg.

Per serving (scant ½ cup): 202 Cal, 2 g Fat, 1 g Sat Fat, 0 g Trans Fat, 5 mg Chol, 213 mg Sod, 43 g Carb, 3 g Fib, 4 g Prot, 79 mg Calc. *PointsPlus* value: **5.**

Vanilla Yogurt and Anisette-Toast Parfaits

SERVES 4

8 anisette toasts, broken into
bite-size pieces

2 (8-ounce) containers vanilla fat-
free yogurt

1 cup thawed frozen light
whipped topping

Put ¼ cup of the toast pieces in the bottom of each of 4 glasses. Layer with ¼ cup of the yogurt, 2 tablespoons of the whipped topping, another ¼ cup of the toast pieces, and another ¼ cup of the yogurt. Top each with another 2 tablespoons of the whipped topping.

Per serving (1 parfait): 163 Cal, 1 g Fat, 0 g Sat Fat, 0 g Trans Fats, 25 mg Chol, 173 mg Sod, 32 g Carb, 0 g Fib, 5 g Prot, 147 mg Calc. *PointsPlus* value: **4.**

⊕ Time-Saver

To break up the anisette toasts quickly, place them in a zip-close plastic bag, then gently pound with a rolling pin or the bottom of a small saucepan until the pieces are bite size.

Fresh Fruit Gazpacho

SERVES 4

½ chilled medium honeydew melon, peeled, seeded, and coarsely chopped (5 cups)

2 chilled apples, peeled, cored, and coarsely chopped

¼ cup lightly packed fresh mint leaves

1 teaspoon grated lemon zest

2 tablespoons lemon juice

2 tablespoons sugar

6 strawberries, hulled and cut into ¼-inch dice

Put about half of the melon into a food processor and puree. Transfer to a large bowl. Combine all the remaining ingredients except the strawberries in the food processor and pulse until chopped. Add to the melon puree and stir to combine. Ladle evenly into 4 chilled soup bowls. Sprinkle evenly with the strawberries and serve at once.

Per serving (about 2 cups): 182 Cal, 1 g Fat, 0 g Sat Fat, 0 g Trans Fat, 0 mg Chol, 25 mg Sod, 47 g Carb, 3 g Fib, 2 g Prot, 32 mg Calc. *PointsPlus* value: **3**.

Five Fruit Salad

SERVES 4

2 cups cubed peeled pitted mango

2 cups cubed honeydew melon

1 cup cubed peeled seeded papaya

1 cup strawberries, hulled and halved

2 (8-ounce) cans pineapple chunks in juice, drained

2 tablespoons thinly sliced fresh basil

2 tablespoons thinly sliced fresh mint

2 tablespoons lime juice

2 teaspoons packed brown sugar

Toss together all the ingredients in a serving bowl until well combined.

Per serving (2 cups): 163 Cal, 1 g Fat, 0 g Sat Fat, 0 g Trans Fat, 0 mg Chol, 20 mg Sod, 42 g Carb, 4 g Fib, 2 g Prot, 40 mg Calc. *PointsPlus* value: **5.**

Watermelon Salad with Mint and Lime

SERVES 4

½ cup sugar

½ cup water

3 tablespoons lime juice

2 tablespoons chopped fresh
  mint

2 teaspoons grated lime zest

6 cups seedless watermelon
  chunks

1 Combine the sugar, water, and lime juice in a small saucepan and set over high heat. Bring to a boil and cook until the sugar dissolves and the mixture is syrupy, about 5 minutes. Remove the saucepan from the heat and stir in the mint and lime zest; let stand about until cool, about 5 minutes.

2 Put the watermelon in a large bowl. Pour the sugar syrup over and toss well.

Per serving (1½ cups): 182 Cal, 1 g Fat, 0 g Sat Fat, 0 g Trans Fat, 0 mg Chol, 21 mg Sod, 46 g Carb, 2 g Fib, 2 g Prot, 25 mg Calc. *PointsPlus* value: **4.**

Tropical Fruit Salad with Toasted Coconut

SERVES 8

- 1 (20-ounce) can pineapple chunks in juice, drained
- 1 (15-ounce) can mandarin oranges in light syrup, drained
- 2 small bananas, sliced
- 2 kiwi fruit, peeled, halved lengthwise, and sliced
- 3 (6-ounce) containers raspberries
- ¼ cup light pancake syrup
- ½ cup sweetened flaked coconut, toasted

Combine all the ingredients except the coconut in a serving bowl. Sprinkle with the coconut and serve at once or refrigerate, covered, up to 6 hours.

Per serving (1 cup): 162 Cal, 2 g Fat, 1 g Sat Fat, 0 g Trans Fat, 0 mg Chol, 21 mg Sod, 38 g Carb, 4 g Fib, 1 g Prot, 25 mg Calc. *PointsPlus* value: **5.**

⏱ Time-Saver

To toast the coconut, spread it on a microwavable plate and microwave on High 1–2 minutes, tossing with a fork every 30 seconds.

Strawberry-Vanilla Malted

SERVES 4

2 cups strawberry low-fat
   ice cream

1½ cups fat-free milk

2 tablespoons malt powder

2 tablespoons vanilla syrup

Combine all the ingredients in a blender, in batches if necessary, and process until thick and smooth, about 1 minute. Pour into 4 glasses.

Per serving (¾ cup): 184 Cal, 4 g Fat, 2 g Sat Fat, 0 g Trans Fat, 22 mg Chol, 101 mg Sod, 31 g Carb, 0 g Fib, 7 g Prot, 254 mg Calc. *PointsPlus* value: **5.**

⏱ Time-Saver

For quick and easy ice cream scooping, wet the scoop with warm water before digging into the ice-cream carton.

Peach-Strawberry Milk Shakes

SERVES 4

4 large peaches, pitted and
   coarsely chopped (4 cups)

1½ cups frozen strawberries

1 cup vanilla soy milk

1 cup vanilla fat-free yogurt

1 tablespoon sugar

Combine all the ingredients in a blender, in batches if necessary, and process until thick and smooth, about 2 minutes. Pour into 4 glasses.

Per serving (1 cup): 203 Cal, 2 g Fat, 0 g Sat Fat, 0 g Trans Fat, 1 mg Chol, 74 mg Sod, 44 g Carb, 4 g Fib, 6 g Prot, 190 mg Calc. *PointsPlus* value: **4.**

⏱ Time-Saver

Use 4 cups frozen sliced peaches instead of fresh.

Chocolate-Raspberry Cooler

SERVES 4

1 pint chocolate fat-free frozen yogurt

½ cup low-fat (1%) milk

½ cup raspberries

2 tablespoons vanilla syrup

6 ice cubes

Combine all the ingredients in a blender, in batches if necessary, and process until smooth, about 2 minutes. Pour into 4 glasses.

Per serving (⅔ cup): 132 Cal, 0 g Fat, 0 g Sat Fat, 0 g Trans Fat, 1 mg Chol, 90 mg Sod, 28 g Carb, 2 g Fib, 4 g Prot, 491 mg Calc. *PointsPlus* value: **3.**

Microwave Spiced Popcorn—Dried Fruit Mix

SERVES 8

1 tablespoon canola oil

¾ teaspoon curry powder

½ teaspoon ground cumin

½ teaspoon paprika

6 cups plain air-popped popcorn

½ cup mixed dried fruit morsels

⅓ cup dry-roasted peanuts

1 Combine the oil, curry powder, cumin, and paprika in a microwavable cup. Microwave on High until fragrant, 45–60 seconds.

2 Combine the popcorn, dried fruit, and peanuts in a serving bowl. Drizzle with the spiced oil and toss to coat evenly.

Per serving (¾ cup): 94 Cal, 5 g Fat, 1 g Sat Fat, 0 g Trans Fat, 0 mg Chol, 51 mg Sod, 11 g Carb, 2 g Fib, 2 g Prot, 10 mg Calc. *PointsPlus* value: **3.**

Chili-Rubbed Flank Steak with BBQ Onions

SERVES 4 (PLUS LEFTOVER STEAK)

2 red onions, sliced

¼ cup ketchup

2 tablespoons water

1 tablespoon apple-cider vinegar

3 teaspoons packed brown sugar

1 tablespoon chili powder

2 teaspoons ground cumin

¾ teaspoon salt

1 (2-pound) flank steak, trimmed

2 zucchini, cut on the diagonal into ¾-inch slices

1 Spray a large nonstick skillet with nonstick spray and set over medium heat. Add the onions and cook, stirring frequently, until softened, about 8 minutes. Stir in the ketchup, water, vinegar, and 1 teaspoon of the brown sugar; simmer until the flavors are blended, about 5 minutes.

2 Meanwhile, spray the rack of a broiler pan with nonstick spray and preheat the broiler.

3 Combine the remaining 2 teaspoons brown sugar, the chili powder, cumin, and ½ teaspoon of the salt in a small bowl. Rub the spice mixture on the steak.

4 Place the steak on the broiler rack. Arrange the zucchini slices around the steak and sprinkle with the remaining ¼ teaspoon salt. Broil 5 inches from the heat until an instant-read thermometer inserted into the side of the steak registers 145°F for medium and the zucchini is tender, about 5 minutes on each side.

5 Cut the steak crosswise in half. Wrap one piece in foil and refrigerate up to 3 days to use for the Beef and Bean Soft Tacos (opposite page). Slice the remaining piece of steak across the grain into thin slices. Serve topped with the onions and zucchini.

Per serving (about 3 slices steak, ⅓ cup onions, and 3 slices zucchini): 248 Cal, 5 g Fat, 2 g Sat Fat, 0 g Trans Fat, 82 mg Chol, 526 mg Sod, 15 g Carb, 3 g Fib, 35 g Prot, 44 mg Calc. **PointsPlus** value: **6.**

Beef and Bean Soft Tacos

SERVES 6

1 small Hass avocado, halved, pitted, and peeled

1½ teaspoons lime juice

1 teaspoon minced pickled jalapeño pepper

⅛ teaspoon salt

1 (15½-ounce) can black beans, rinsed and drained

1½ cups prepared thick and chunky salsa

Reserved steak from **Chili-Rubbed Flank Steak with BBQ Onions** (opposite page)

6 (7-inch) whole-wheat tortillas, warmed

1 tomato, diced

1 cup shredded romaine lettuce

1 With a fork, coarsely mash the avocado in a small bowl. Stir in the lime juice, pickled jalapeño, and salt; set aside.

2 Combine the beans and salsa in a large skillet; bring to a simmer over medium-low heat. Simmer, stirring occasionally, until heated through, about 5 minutes.

3 Meanwhile, slice the steak across the grain into thin slices. Add to the bean mixture and cook, stirring, until heated through, about 2 minutes. Spoon the beef and bean mixture evenly along the center of each tortilla. Top each with about 2 tablespoons of the tomato, 2 tablespoons of the lettuce, and 2 tablespoons of the mashed avocado. Fold the two opposite sides of each tortilla over to enclose the filling.

Per serving (1 taco): 325 Cal, 8 g Fat, 2 g Sat Fat, 0 g Trans Fat, 54 mg Chol, 914 mg Sod, 35 g Carb, 11 g Fib, 30 g Prot, 75 mg Calc. **PointsPlus** value: **8.**

Honey-Spice Pork

SERVES 4 (PLUS LEFTOVER PORK)

1 (9-ounce) package frozen
  Italian green beans

1 (10-ounce) package frozen corn
  kernels

2½ teaspoons Cajun seasoning

¼ teaspoon salt

⅛ teaspoon dried thyme

1 cup grape tomatoes, halved

8 (5-ounce) boneless pork chops,
  ¾ inch thick, trimmed

¼ cup water

2 tablespoons honey

1 Combine the green beans, corn, ¼ teaspoon of the Cajun seasoning, the salt, and thyme in a large microwavable bowl. Cover and microwave on High 3 minutes. Stir, then microwave on High until tender, about 2 minutes. Stir in the tomatoes and microwave until softened, about 1 minute longer. Set aside.

2 Meanwhile, sprinkle the pork chops with 2 teaspoons of the Cajun seasoning. Spray 2 large nonstick skillets with nonstick spray and set over medium-high heat. Add 4 chops to each skillet and reduce the heat to medium. Cook until an instant-read thermometer inserted into the side of a chop registers 160°F for medium, about 4 minutes on each side; transfer the chops to a plate and keep warm.

3 Add the water, honey, and the remaining ¼ teaspoon Cajun seasoning to one of the skillets. Cook, stirring to scrape up any brown bits from the bottom of the pan, until the pan sauce thickens slightly, about 2 minutes. Return 4 chops to the skillet and turn to coat with the sauce. Serve with the vegetables.

4 Put the remaining 4 pork chops in an airtight container and refrigerate up to 3 days to use for the Open-Face BBQ Pork Sandwiches with Pineapple Slaw (opposite page).

Per serving (1 pork chop, 1 tablespoon sauce, and 1 cup vegetables): 336 Cal, 11 g Fat, 4 g Sat Fat, 0 g Trans Fat, 87 mg Chol, 407 mg Sod, 27 g Carb, 4 g Fib, 33 g Prot, 39 mg Calc. *PointsPlus* value: **8.**

Open-Face BBQ Pork Sandwiches with Pineapple Slaw

SERVES 4

2 tablespoons fat-free mayonnaise

1 tablespoon apple-cider vinegar

¼ teaspoon salt

4 cups packaged coleslaw mix

½ cup canned drained pineapple tidbits

½ red bell pepper, chopped

1 scallion, thinly sliced

Reserved pork chops from **Honey-Spice Pork** (opposite page)

¾ cup fat-free barbecue sauce

2 whole-wheat hamburger buns, split

1 Combine the mayonnaise, vinegar, and salt in a serving bowl. Add the coleslaw mix, pineapple, bell pepper, and scallion; toss to mix. Set aside.

2 Thinly slice the pork chops. Combine the pork and barbecue sauce in a medium saucepan and set over medium heat. Bring to a simmer and cook, covered, stirring occasionally, until heated through, about 5 minutes. Place a bun half on each of 4 plates. Pile the pork and sauce evenly on each bun half. Serve with the slaw.

Per serving (1 sandwich and generous 1 cup slaw): 405 Cal, 12 g Fat, 4 g Sat Fat, 0 g Trans Fat, 88 mg Chol, 1012 mg Sod, 40 g Carb, 3 g Fib, 33 g Prot, 98 mg Calc. *PointsPlus* value: **10.**

⏱ Time-Saver

Serve a dish of no-sugar-added pickles alongside the sandwiches.

Tunisian Lamb Chops

SERVES 4 (PLUS LEFTOVER LAMB CHOPS)

1 garlic clove, minced

1 teaspoon ground cumin

½ teaspoon ground coriander

¼ teaspoon salt

¼ teaspoon black pepper

⅛ teaspoon cayenne

8 (5-ounce) lamb loin chops, trimmed

4 large plum tomatoes, halved lengthwise

1 (10-ounce) bag spinach

2 tablespoons chopped fresh mint

1 Spray the rack of a broiler pan with nonstick spray and preheat the broiler.

2 Combine the garlic, cumin, coriander, salt, pepper, and cayenne in a small bowl. Rub the spice mixture on 4 of the lamb chops. Place all 8 lamb chops on the broiler rack. Broil 5 inches from the heat 4 minutes. Turn the chops.

3 Place the tomato halves, cut side up, alongside the chops. Broil until an instant-read thermometer inserted into the side of a chop registers 145°F for medium and the tomatoes begin to soften, 4–5 minutes longer. Place the plain chops in an airtight container and refrigerate up to 3 days to use for the Hearty Lamb and White Bean Stew (opposite page).

4 Meanwhile, microwave the spinach according to the package directions. Sprinkle the chops with the mint and serve with the tomatoes and spinach.

Per serving (1 lamb chop, 1 tomato, and ¾ cup spinach): 142 Cal, 6 g Fat, 2 g Sat Fat, 0 g Trans Fat, 52 mg Chol, 168 mg Sod, 5 g Carb, 2 g Fib, 18 g Prot, 79 mg Calc. *PointsPlus* value: **4.**

◆ Filling Extra

A side of whole wheat couscous is a tasty and traditional way to serve these North African lamb chops (½ cup cooked whole wheat couscous per serving will increase the *PointsPlus* value by **3**).

Hearty Lamb and White Bean Stew

SERVES 4

1 teaspoon olive oil

1 small onion, chopped

2 garlic cloves, crushed through a press

½ teaspoon dried rosemary

2 (15½-ounce) cans cannellini (white kidney) beans, rinsed and drained

1 (14½-ounce) can stewed tomatoes

½ cup water

Reserved lamb chops from **Tunisian Lamb Chops** (opposite page)

2 tablespoons chopped flat-leaf parsley

1 Heat the oil in a large saucepan over medium heat. Add the onion, garlic, and rosemary; cook, stirring, until softened, about 2 minutes. Add the beans, tomatoes, and water; bring to a boil over medium-high heat. Reduce the heat and simmer, covered, breaking up the tomatoes with a wooden spoon, until slightly thickened, about 8 minutes.

2 Meanwhile, remove the lamb meat from the bones; discard the bones. Cut the lamb into ¾-inch chunks. Add to the bean mixture and cook, stirring, until heated through, about 2 minutes. Sprinkle with the parsley.

Per serving (1 ¼ cups): 363 Cal, 7 g Fat, 2 g Sat Fat, 0 g Trans Fat, 52 mg Chol, 725 mg Sod, 44 g Carb, 11 g Fib, 32 g Prot, 187 mg Calc. *PointsPlus* value: **9.**

Basque Chicken Stew

SERVES 4 (PLUS LEFTOVER CHICKEN AND VEGETABLES)

4 teaspoons olive oil

2 pounds chicken tenders

½ teaspoon salt

1 large onion, sliced

2 large different-colored bell peppers, cut into strips

1 teaspoon salt-free garlic and herb seasoning

1 (14½-ounce) can diced fire-roasted tomatoes

¼ cup pimento-stuffed green olives, coarsely chopped

1 teaspoon sugar

4 Canadian bacon slices, cut into strips

1 Heat 2 teaspoons of the oil in each of 2 large skillets over medium-high heat. Sprinkle the chicken with the salt. Add half of the chicken to each skillet; top evenly with the onion and bell peppers and sprinkle with the herb seasoning.

2 Cook, stirring the vegetables occasionally and turning the chicken once, until the vegetables are softened and the chicken is cooked through, about 8 minutes. Remove one of the skillets from the heat and set aside. Add the tomatoes, olives, and sugar to the remaining skillet and bring to a boil. Reduce the heat and simmer, partially covered, until the vegetables are tender, about 6 minutes. Add the Canadian bacon.

3 Transfer the reserved chicken and vegetables to an airtight container and refrigerate up to 2 days to use for the Louisiana Po'boys (opposite page).

Per serving (about 1 ⅓ cups stew): 250 Cal, 9 g Fat, 2 g Sat Fat, 0 g Trans Fat, 81 mg Chol, 826 mg Sod, 10 g Carb, 2 g Fib, 32 g Prot, 62 mg Calc. **PointsPlus** value: **6.**

⏱ Time-Saver

Save on prep time by using 2 cups sliced onion and 3 cups sliced bell peppers from a salad bar.

Louisiana Po'boys

SERVES 4

⅓ cup fat-free mayonnaise

1 scallion, chopped

1 tablespoon coarse-grained Dijon mustard

1 tablespoon ketchup

¼ teaspoon Cajun seasoning

Reserved chicken and vegetables from **Basque Chicken Stew** (opposite page)

4 (2½-ounce) rectangular rolls, split

2 cups shredded romaine lettuce

1 tomato, cut into 8 slices

1 Combine the mayonnaise, scallion, mustard, ketchup, and Cajun seasoning in a small bowl. Cut the chicken into bite-size chunks. Put the chicken and vegetables on a microwavable plate; cover with a vented piece of plastic wrap and microwave on High until heated through, 2–3 minutes.

2 Spread the mayonnaise mixture evenly on the cut sides of the rolls. Layer the bottom of each roll with ½ cup of the lettuce, one-fourth of the chicken and vegetable mixture, and 2 tomato slices. Cover with the tops of the rolls.

Per serving (1 sandwich): 421 Cal, 10 g Fat, 2 g Sat Fat, 0 g Trans Fat, 71 mg Chol, 928 mg Sod, 48 g Carb, 4 g Fib, 34 g Prot, 109 mg Calc. ***PointsPlus*** value: **10.**

◆ *Filling Extra*

For a healthy alternative to the classic side of potato chips or fries, serve this traditional sandwich with carrot and celery sticks.

Kielbasa with Peppers and Onions

SERVES 4 (PLUS LEFTOVER SAUSAGE, PEPPERS, AND ONIONS)

1½ pounds reduced-fat turkey kielbasa, cut into 2-inch chunks

1 large red bell pepper, cut into 4 slabs

1 large green bell pepper, cut into 4 slabs

1 large onion, sliced

1½ teaspoons olive oil

½ (1¼-pound) bag refrigerated shredded hash brown potatoes

1 cup shredded fat-free mozzarella cheese

1 garlic clove, minced

2 large plum tomatoes, chopped

1½ teaspoons balsamic vinegar

1 Spray the rack of a broiler pan with nonstick spray and preheat the broiler.

2 Place the sausage, peppers, and onion on the broiler rack and spray with nonstick spray. Broil 5 inches from the heat until the sausage is browned and the vegetables are tender, about 4 minutes on each side. Transfer half of the sausage and pepper mixture to an airtight container and refrigerate up to 3 days to use for the Sausage and Red Bean Gumbo (opposite page).

3 Meanwhile, heat 1 teaspoon of the oil in a medium nonstick skillet over medium heat. Add the potatoes, pressing with a spatula to form a flat cake. Cook until browned on the bottom, about 4 minutes. Turn the potato cake, then cut into 4 wedges with the edge of the spatula. Cook until browned, about 4 minutes longer. Sprinkle with the mozzarella; cover the skillet and remove from the heat.

4 Heat the remaining ½ teaspoon oil with the garlic in a small saucepan over low heat. Stir in the tomatoes and cook until softened, about 3 minutes. Stir in the vinegar. Put a potato wedge on each of 4 plates; top evenly with the sausage and pepper mixture and the tomato sauce.

Per serving (¼ of sausage and pepper mixture, 1 potato wedge, and about 3 tablespoons tomato sauce): 266 Cal, 10 g Fat, 3 g Sat Fat, 0 g Trans Fat, 49 mg Chol, 1285 mg Sod, 21 g Carb, 2 g Fib, 22 g Prot, 270 mg Calc. *PointsPlus* value: **7.**

Sausage and Red Bean Gumbo

SERVES 4

Reserved sausage and peppers from **Kielbasa with Peppers and Onions** (opposite page)

1 (15½-ounce) can red kidney beans, rinsed and drained

1 (14½-ounce) can no-salt added diced tomatoes

2 cups water

2 celery stalks, chopped

1 teaspoon Cajun seasoning

2 cups hot cooked quick-cooking brown rice

2 scallions, thinly sliced

1 Thinly slice the chunks of sausage and chop the peppers and onions. Combine the sausage, peppers, onions, beans, tomatoes, water, celery, and Cajun seasoning in a large saucepan and bring to a boil over medium-high heat. Reduce the heat and simmer, partially covered, stirring occasionally, until the flavors are blended, about 10 minutes.

2 Transfer 1 cup of the gumbo to a blender and puree; stir the puree into the gumbo. Put ½ cup of the rice in each of 4 shallow bowls. Top evenly with the gumbo and sprinkle with the scallions.

Per serving (½ cup rice and about 1 ¾ cups gumbo): 384 Cal, 10 g Fat, 2 g Sat Fat, 0 g Trans Fat, 44 mg Chol, 1242 mg Sod, 51 g Carb, 12 g Fib, 24 g Prot, 106 mg Calc. *PointsPlus* value: **10.**

Mustard-Glazed Salmon with Lemony Potatoes and Snap Pea Salad

SERVES 4 (PLUS LEFTOVER SALMON)

1 pound baby red potatoes, halved or quartered if large

¼ cup fat-free mayonnaise

1 tablespoon coarse-grained Dijon mustard

½ teaspoon salt

½ small English (seedless) cucumber, diced

1 cup sugar snap peas, strings removed

2 tablespoons chopped red onion

2 tablespoons unseasoned rice vinegar

6 (6-ounce) salmon steaks, 1 inch thick

1½ teaspoons olive oil

½ teaspoon grated lemon zest

1 Put the potatoes in a medium saucepan and add enough water to cover; bring to a boil over medium-high heat. Reduce the heat and simmer, covered, until tender, about 8 minutes; drain.

2 Meanwhile, spray the rack of a broiler pan with olive oil nonstick spray and preheat the broiler.

3 Combine the mayonnaise, mustard, and ⅛ teaspoon of the salt in a small bowl; set aside. Combine the cucumber, snap peas, onion, vinegar, and ⅛ teaspoon of the salt in a serving bowl; set aside.

4 Place the salmon steaks on the broiler rack and broil 5 inches from the heat 4 minutes. Turn and broil 2 minutes longer. Spread the mustard mixture evenly over 4 of the steaks. Broil until the salmon is just opaque in the center and the topping is lightly browned, about 2 minutes longer. Put the 2 plain salmon steaks on a plate; cover tightly and refrigerate up to 2 days to use for the Chunky Salmon Salad (page 318).

5 Toss together the potatoes, oil, lemon zest, and the remaining ¼ teaspoon salt. Serve the salmon with the potatoes and snap pea salad.

Per serving (1 salmon steak, ¾ cup potatoes, generous ½ cup salad): 337 Cal, 11 g Fat, 3 g Sat Fat, 0 g Trans Fat, 97 mg Chol, 603 mg Sod, 25 g Carb, 4 g Fib, 33 g Prot, 59 mg Calc. **PointsPlus** value: **8.**

⏱ Time-Saver

Use ½ teaspoon lemon and pepper seasoning instead of the lemon zest and salt.

Mustard-Glazed Salmon with Lemony Potatoes and Snap Pea Salad

Lemon and Herb Crumb—Topped Cod

SERVES 4 (PLUS LEFTOVER COD)

1 garlic clove, peeled

2 slices whole-wheat bread, torn into 1-inch pieces

2 tablespoons lightly packed flat-leaf parsley leaves

½ teaspoon grated lemon zest

2 teaspoons olive oil

¼ teaspoon salt

2 tablespoons plain fat-free yogurt

2 teaspoons lemon juice

1 (3-pound) cod fillet, cut into 8 equal pieces

1 (16-ounce) package frozen stir-fry vegetables

1 Put the garlic into a food processor and pulse until finely chopped. Add the bread and parsley; pulse until crumbs form and the parsley is chopped. Add the lemon zest, 1 teaspoon of the oil, and ⅛ teaspoon of the salt; pulse to combine. Transfer to a small bowl; set aside.

2 Combine the yogurt, lemon juice, and the remaining ⅛ teaspoon salt in a small bowl; set aside.

3 Spray the rack of a broiler pan with nonstick spray and preheat the broiler. Place the cod on the rack and broil 5 inches from the heat 4 minutes. Turn and broil until just opaque in the center, about 3 minutes longer.

4 Transfer the plain pieces of cod to an airtight container and refrigerate up to 2 days to use for the New England Fish Chowder (opposite page). Spread the yogurt mixture evenly over the remaining 4 pieces of the cod and sprinkle evenly with the bread crumb mixture, pressing lightly so it adheres. Lightly spray the crumbs with nonstick spray. Broil until the crumbs are browned, about 1 minute. Transfer the crumb-topped cod to a platter; keep warm.

5 Heat the remaining 1 teaspoon oil in a large nonstick skillet over medium-high heat. Add the frozen vegetables and stir-fry until tender-crisp, 4–5 minutes. Serve with the cod.

Per serving (1 piece cod and ¾ cup vegetables): 255 Cal, 5 g Fat, 1 g Sat Fat, 0 g Trans Fat, 90 mg Chol, 370 mg Sod, 15 g Carb, 4 g Fib, 37 g Prot, 90 mg Calc. *PointsPlus* value: **5.**

New England Fish Chowder

SERVES 4

2 (8-ounce) bottles clam juice

1 onion, chopped

1 celery stalk, chopped

1 (15½-ounce) can cannellini (white kidney) beans, rinsed and drained

1 (14½-ounce) can diced new potatoes, rinsed and drained

1 cup frozen corn kernels

½ teaspoon dried thyme

½ teaspoon salt

¼ teaspoon black pepper

Leftover cod from **Lemon and Herb Crumb–Topped Cod** (opposite page)

¾ cup fat-free half-and-half

1   Put the clam juice, onion, and celery in a large saucepan and bring to a boil over medium-high heat. Cook, covered, about 1 minute. Add the beans, potatoes, corn, thyme, salt, and pepper; bring to a boil. Reduce the heat and simmer, covered, about 10 minutes.

2   Meanwhile, break the cod into large chunks.

3   With the back of a spoon, mash about one-third of the bean and potato mixture. Add the cod and half-and-half to the chowder. Reduce the heat to low and simmer very gently until heated through, about 4 minutes.

Per serving (generous 1½ cups chowder): 380 Cal, 3 g Fat, 1 g Sat Fat, 0 g Trans Fat, 96 mg Chol, 1154 mg Sod, 44 g Carb, 8 g Fib, 43 g Prot, 168 mg Calc. *PointsPlus* value: **8.**

Polenta with Chunky Mushroom-Zucchini Ragu

SERVES 4 (PLUS LEFTOVER POLENTA)

7 cups water

¾ teaspoon salt

1½ cups instant polenta

2 teaspoons olive oil

1 (10-ounce) package sliced cremini or white mushrooms

1 large zucchini, quartered lengthwise and sliced

2 garlic cloves, minced

2 tablespoons tomato paste

8 pitted kalamata olives, coarsely chopped

⅓ cup grated Parmesan cheese

½ cup shredded part-skim mozzarella cheese

1 Line a 9 x 13-inch baking dish with foil, allowing the foil to extend over the rim of the pan by 2 inches; spray with nonstick spray.

2 Meanwhile, bring 6 cups of the water and ½ teaspoon of the salt to a boil in a large pot over high heat. Gradually whisk in the polenta, then reduce the heat and cook, stirring constantly with a wooden spoon, until thickened, 4–5 minutes. Remove the pot from the heat. Transfer 3 cups of the polenta to the baking dish, spreading it evenly. Cover tightly with plastic wrap and refrigerate up to 3 days to use for the Polenta Lasagna (opposite page).

3 To make the ragu, heat the oil in a large nonstick skillet over medium-high heat. Add the mushrooms and cook, stirring, until lightly browned, about 4 minutes. Stir in the zucchini, garlic, tomato paste, ½ cup of the water, and the remaining ¼ teaspoon salt. Reduce the heat and simmer, stirring, until the zucchini is tender, about 5 minutes. Stir in the olives and remove the skillet from the heat.

4 Set the pot of polenta over medium-high heat. Whisk in the remaining ½ cup water and bring to a simmer. Remove the pot from the heat and stir in the Parmesan. Spoon the polenta evenly into 4 bowls; top evenly with the ragu and sprinkle with the mozzarella.

Per serving (¾ cup polenta, ¾ cup ragu, and 2 tablespoons mozzarella): 246 Cal, 9 g Fat, 4 g Sat Fat, 0 g Trans Fats, 14 mg Chol, 843 mg Sod, 31 g Carb, 4 g Fib, 13 g Prot, 352 mg Calc. **PointsPlus** value: **7.**

Polenta Lasagna

SERVES 4

1 (10-ounce) bag baby spinach

1 cup shredded part-skim
mozzarella cheese

4 tablespoons grated Parmesan
cheese

¾ cup fat-free ricotta cheese

Reserved Polenta from **Polenta
with Chunky Mushroom-
Zucchini Ragu** (opposite page)

1½ cups fat-free marinara sauce

1 Microwave the spinach according to the package directions. Drain in a colander, then rinse under cold water; squeeze out the excess moisture. Combine ½ cup of the mozzarella and 2 tablespoons of the Parmesan in a small bowl; set aside. Combine the spinach, the remaining ½ cup mozzarella and 2 tablespoons Parmesan, and the ricotta in a medium bowl; set aside.

2 Lift the polenta from the baking dish using the foil ends as handles. Cut lengthwise in half then crosswise in quarters to make a total of 8 rectangles.

3 Spray the same baking dish with nonstick spray. Arrange 4 polenta rectangles in the dish in a single layer. Spoon 3 tablespoons of the marinara sauce over each; top evenly with the spinach-ricotta mixture. Cover with the remaining pieces of polenta. Spoon 3 tablespoons of the remaining marinara sauce over each piece of polenta and sprinkle with the reserved mozzarella mixture.

4 Spray a piece of plastic wrap with nonstick spray and use it to loosely cover the lasagna. Microwave on High until heated through and bubbly, 5–7 minutes.

Per serving (1 rectangle of lasagna): 320 Cal, 8 g Fat, 5 g Sat Fat, 0 g Trans Fat, 24 mg Chol, 919 mg Sod, 42 g Carb, 4 g Fib, 22 g Prot, 584 mg Calc. *PointsPlus* value: **7.**

Veggie Bean Chili

SERVES 4 (PLUS LEFTOVER VEGETABLE MIXTURE)

1 teaspoon olive oil

1 onion, chopped

2 garlic cloves, minced

2 cups mixed vegetable juice

1 (28-ounce) can diced tomatoes

2 (15½-ounce) cans beans, such as red kidney and chickpeas, rinsed and drained

1 (16-ounce) package frozen vegetable blend, such as carrots, corn, and green beans

1½ teaspoons chili powder

½ teaspoon ground cumin

¼ cup reduced-fat shredded cheddar cheese

¼ cup fat-free sour cream

1 Heat the oil in a large pot over medium heat. Add the onion and garlic; cook, stirring, until softened, about 2 minutes. Add the vegetable juice, tomatoes with their juice, the beans, and vegetables; bring to a boil over medium-high heat. Reduce the heat and simmer, covered, until the vegetables are tender, about 8 minutes.

2 Transfer 3 cups of the vegetable mixture to an airtight container and refrigerate up to 3 days to use for the Moroccan Vegetable Tagine (opposite page).

3 Add the chili powder and cumin to the chili in the pot. Simmer, covered, until the flavors blend, about 5 minutes. Spoon the chili evenly into 4 bowls and top evenly with the cheddar and sour cream.

Per serving (generous 1 cup chili, 1 tablespoon cheddar, and 1 tablespoon sour cream): 280 Cal, 3 g Fat, 1 g Sat Fat, 0 g Trans Fat, 3 mg Chol, 795 mg Sod, 50 g Carb, 14 g Fib, 15 g Prot, 208 mg Calc. *PointsPlus* value: **5.**

◆ Filling Extra

Spoon this flavorful chili over brown rice (½ cup cooked brown rice per serving will increase the *PointsPlus* value by **3**).

Moroccan Vegetable Tagine

SERVES 4

1¾ cups water

1 cup whole-wheat couscous

¼ teaspoon salt

1 (14½-ounce) can vegetable broth

1 (1-pound) bag cut up butternut squash, cut into 1-inch chunks

Reserved vegetables from **Veggie Bean Chili** (opposite page)

¼ cup dried cranberries

1 teaspoon ground cumin

1 teaspoon curry powder

⅛ teaspoon cinnamon

1 cup frozen peas

¼ cup chopped fresh cilantro

1 Bring 1¼ cups of the water to a boil in a small saucepan. Stir in the couscous and salt; remove the saucepan from the heat. Let stand 5 minutes, then fluff with a fork. Set aside.

2 Meanwhile, put the remaining ½ cup water, the broth, and squash in a large skillet and bring to a boil over medium-high heat. Add the reserved vegetables, the dried cranberries, cumin, curry powder, and cinnamon to the pan and stir to combine. Return to a boil; reduce the heat and simmer, covered, until the squash is almost tender, about 8 minutes. Add the peas and cook, covered, until the squash is tender, about 2 minutes longer; sprinkle with the cilantro. Serve over the couscous.

Per serving (1½ cups tagine and ⅔ cup couscous): 318 Cal, 3 g Fat, 0 g Sat Fat, 0 g Trans Fats, 0 mg Chol, 853 mg Sod, 66 g Carb, 14 g Fib, 13 g Prot, 144 mg Calc. *PointsPlus* value: **8**.

◆ Filling Extra

Top each serving of this warmly spiced stew with a ¼-cup dollop of plain fat-free sour cream. This will increase the per-serving *PointsPlus* value by **1**.

Dry and Liquid Measurements

If you are converting the recipes in this book to metric measurements, use the following chart as a guide.

Teaspoons	Tablespoons	Cups	Fluid Ounces
3 teaspoons	1 tablespoon		½ fluid ounce
6 teaspoons	2 tablespoons	⅛ cup	1 fluid ounce
8 teaspoons	2 tablespoons plus 2 teaspoons	⅙ cup	
12 teaspoons	4 tablespoons	¼ cup	2 fluid ounces
15 teaspoons	5 tablespoons	⅓ cup minus 1 teaspoon	
16 teaspoons	5 tablespoons plus 1 teaspoon	⅓ cup	
18 teaspoons	6 tablespoons	¼ cup plus 2 tablespoons	3 fluid ounces
24 teaspoons	8 tablespoons	½ cup	4 fluid ounces
30 teaspoons	10 tablespoons	½ cup plus 2 tablespoons	5 fluid ounces
32 teaspoons	10 tablespoons plus 2 teaspoons	⅔ cup	
36 teaspoons	12 tablespoons	¾ cup	6 fluid ounces
42 teaspoons	14 tablespoons	1 cup minus 2 tablespoons	7 fluid ounces
45 teaspoons	15 tablespoons	1 cup minus 1 tablespoon	
48 teaspoons	16 tablespoons	1 cup	8 fluid ounces

Length	
1 inch	25 millimeters
1 inch	2.5 centimeters

Weight	
1 ounce	30 grams
¼ pound	120 grams
½ pound	240 grams
1 pound	480 grams

Oven Temperature	
250°F	120°C
275°F	140°C
300°F	150°C
325°F	160°C
350°F	180°C
375°F	190°C
400°F	200°C
425°F	220°C
450°F	230°C
475°F	250°C
500°F	260°C
525°F	270°C

Volume	
¼ teaspoon	1 milliliter
½ teaspoon	2 milliliters
1 teaspoon	5 milliliters
1 tablespoon	15 milliliters
2 tablespoons	30 milliliters
3 tablespoons	45 milliliters
¼ cup	60 milliliters
⅓ cup	80 milliliters
½ cup	120 milliliters
⅔ cup	160 milliliters
¾ cup	175 milliliters
1 cup	240 milliliters
1 quart	950 milliliters

NOTE: Measurement of less than ⅛ teaspoon is considered a dash or a pinch.
Metric volume measurements are approximate.

Index

329

Index

Index

333

Recipes by *PointsPlus* value

Pork Tenderloin with Cranberry Pan Sauce and Butternut Squash, 110
Pork with Cauliflower and Walnuts, 108
Pork, Orange, and Fennel Salad, 46
Portobello Mushroom–Garlic Burgers, 234
Potato Pierogies with Wild Mushroom Sauce, 277
Roast Beef and Watercress Sandwiches, 60
Sausage and Onion Fajitas, 162
Sausage, Mushroom, and Tomato Stew, 264
Sautéed Chicken with White Wine and Mushrooms, 257
Scallops with Garlic Bread Crumbs, 274
Scrambled Eggs with Smoked Salmon and Onion, 33
Sea Bass with Green Sauce, 182
Sesame-Crusted Tuna Steaks, 172
Shrimp and Papaya Salad with Honey-Lime Dressing, 55
Sliced Chicken and Smoked Mozzarella Salad, 266
Tofu and Vegetable Lo Mein, 226
Tropical Sorbet Smoothie, 26
Turkey and Corn Quesadillas, 161
Turkey, Potato, and Sage Patties, 42
Warm Lentil Salad with Tahini Dressing, 215

7 *PointsPlus* value
Avocado, Tofu, and Tomato Sandwiches, 71
Beef Skewers with Cilantro and Ginger, 246
Cajun Tuna with Scallion-Caper Mayonnaise, 273
Chicken, White Bean, and Arugula Salad, 136
Corn and Crab Chowder, 81
Curried Vegetables with Lentils and Couscous, 206
Double Chocolate–Cranberry Pudding, 290
Double Mushroom Broth with Soba Noodles, 84
Double Mushroom Burgers with Spiced-up Ketchup, 249
Easy Moussaka, 124
Green Chile Chicken, 308
Grilled Vegetable–Gruyère Sandwiches, 70
Kielbasa with Peppers and Onions, 314
Lebanese Chicken-Pita Salad, 50
Mediterranean-Style Salad Pizzas, 211
Microwave Deviled Chicken, 148
Microwave Salmon Fillet with Lemon Sauce, 271
Mixed Vegetable and Tofu Stir-Fry, 229
North African–Style Burgers, 101
Oatmeal with Dried Fruit and Brown Sugar, 20
Peppered Steak with Brandy-Mustard Sauce, 93
Polenta Lasagna, 323
Polenta with Chunky Mushroom-Zucchini Ragu, 322
Pork Chops with Corn–Bell Pepper Relish, 104

Pressure Cooker Moroccan-Style Lamb, 122
Pressure-Cooked Honey and Spice Porridge, 19
Quick Burgundy-Style Beef Stew, 96
Rich and Creamy Oatmeal with Blueberries and Walnuts, 22
Salmon with Balsamic-Honey Sauce, 270
Salmon with Tomato-Scallion Relish, 272
Sausages and Onion on Crispy Polenta, 150
Sloppy Joes Tex-Mex Style, 146
Spiced Oatmeal Brûlée, 21
Sweet-and-Sour Pineapple Chicken, 261
Swordfish with Asian Flavors, 170
Tilapia and Corn Stew, 187
Vegetable-Topped Orange Couscous, 223
Watercress, Scallop, and Noodle Soup, 198
White Bean Bruschetta with Chopped Salad, 216

8 *PointsPlus* value
Beef and Bean Soft Tacos, 303
Beef and Green Beans with Asian Flavors, 97
Capellini with Mussels in Tomato-Basil Sauce, 200
Chicken and Mushroom Bolognese, 149
Double Cheese and Macaroni, 220
Double Cheese Polenta with Golden Onions, 225
Fruit and Cheese–Stuffed French Toast, 8
Gnocchi with Herb-Walnut Pesto, 219
Honey-Spice Pork, 304
Lemon Pancakes with Fresh Raspberry Sauce, 14
Mixed Berry French Toast, 10
Moroccan Vegetable Tagine, 325
Mustard-Glazed Salmon with Lemony Potatoes and Snap Pea Salad, 316
New England Fish Chowder, 321
Pasta with Red Clam Sauce, 199
Salad-Topped Pork Cutlets, 109
Salmon Salad Sandwiches, 68
Sautéed Pork with Peaches, 113
Shrimp with Bok Choy and Baby Corn, 194
Skillet Pork Chops with Apricot-Mustard Sauce, 107
Smoked Salmon, Dill, and Red Onion Pizzas, 38
Spiced Turkey Burgers with Yogurt and Chutney, 268
Spicy Chicken and Broccoli Stir-Fry, 310
Stir-Fried Chicken and Mushrooms with Cellophane Noodles, 137
Stir-Fried Pork and Broccoli with Hoisin Sauce, 114
Striped Bass with Cherry Tomato–Caper Sauce, 181
Tex-Mex Beef and Vegetable Salad, 103
Turkey, Apple, and Honey-Mustard Wraps, 65
Warm Caesar-Style Chicken Sandwiches, 64

9 *PointsPlus* value
Bread Salad with Tomatoes, Beans, and Feta, 212
Brown Rice and Soy Burritos, 230
Chicken Burgers on Garlic Bread, 262
Fresh Linguine with Sausage and Spinach, 163
Hearty Lamb and White Bean Stew, 307
Herbed Bean and Tomato Pita Pizzas, 208
Hunan-Style Vegetables and Tempeh, 231
Lamb Burgers with Garlicky Yogurt Sauce, 126
Middle Eastern–Style Turkey Burgers, 158
Moroccan-Style Beef Kebabs, 94
Open-Face Chicken, Tomato, and Arugula Panini, 63
Raspberry-Cornmeal Pancakes, 11
Sautéed Bananas with Rum and Brown Sugar, 282
Spinach Fettuccine with Tomato-Soy Ragu, 217
Tempeh and Black Bean Tostadas, 232
Turkey–Green Chile Tacos, 159

10 *PointsPlus* value
Cavatelli with Escarole and White Beans, 204
Louisiana Po' boys, 313
Open-Face BBQ Pork Sandwiches with Pineapple Slaw, 305
Sausage and Red Bean Gumbo, 315
Szechuan Chicken and Bok Choy Stir-Fry, 145

11 *PointsPlus* value
Soy-Glazed Fresh Tuna Sandwiches, 66

Recipes That Work with the Simply Filling technique